MIXED·MEDIA
explorations

BLENDING PAPER, FABRIC, AND EMBELLISHMENT TO CREATE INSPIRED DESIGNS

BERYL TAYLOR

Mixed-Media Explorations
Blending Paper, Fabric, and Embellishment to Create Inspired Designs

© Quilting Arts, LLC & Beryl Taylor

Quilting Arts, LLC
P.O. Box 685
23 Gleasondale Rd.
Stow, MA 01775
www.quiltingartsllc.com

Credits

Publisher: John P. Bolton, Esq.
Editor: Patricia Bolton
Technical Editors: Barbara Delaney & Cate Coulacos Prato
Designer: Larissa Davis
Photographers:
Hornick Rivlin Studios
Korday Studios

Front Cover: (clockwise from upper left)–"Corset," "A is for Always," and "Medieval Book."

For your convenience, the publisher has posted a current listing of corrections on our website at www.quiltingartsllc.com.
If a correction is not already listed, please contact us at info@quiltingartsllc.com or write us at P.O. Box 685, Stow, MA, 01775.

Library of Congress Cataloging-in-publication Data

Library of Congress Control Number: 2006902247

Taylor, Beryl

Mixed-Media Explorations: Blending Paper, Fabric, and Embellishment to Create Inspired Designs

p.cm.

ISBN # 0-9766928-2-1 (paper trade)

1. Textile fabrics. 2. Assemblage (Art). 1. Title.

Printed in China.

TABLE of CONTENTS

DEDICATION

To Vicki, my daughter, who
said over and over again,
"Go for it, Mum."

To my husband Ian, without
whose help and support
I couldn't have completed
this task.

To my son, Matthew, whose
quiet presence and strength
spurred me on.

To Mum—without you,
I wouldn't be here.

To Juan Angela—what would
I do without you?

To friends Allyson, Vivien,
Debbie, and Jan—thanks.

ACKNOWLEDGEMENTS

The idea of me writing a book was quite
intimidating, to say the least, but thanks to
John and Patricia Bolton (and especially
Patricia) who talked me through it and made it
that much easier, I did it. Thank you to their
designer, Larissa Davis, for her talent and
hard work and to Barbara Delaney and Cate
Coulacos Prato of the editorial staff who also
helped edit this book and make it a piece of art.

My deepest thanks to my teacher and mentor,
Joan Archer, who taught me embroidery so
many years ago. Your knowledge and
generosity are greatly appreciated to this day.

Thanks to Vivien Lunniss who taught me so
much about calligraphy and friendship.

And finally, thanks to Allyson who gave her
time to come and play and experiment.

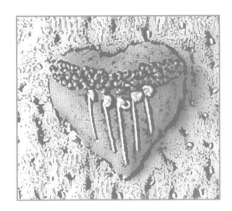

FOREWORD

*E*very once in a while you come across an artist whose work is so compelling, you're desperate to drop everything to study it for days on end. Such was the case when I was first introduced to Beryl Taylor. Three years ago QUILTING ARTS MAGAZINE® hosted a fabric book challenge, and Beryl submitted her highly embellished "Silk Book"—one of the most dazzling, inventive pieces of fabric art I had ever seen. With quilting, beading, and rubberstamping, she created an inviting, magical realm. Page after page, I marveled at the attention to detail and the careful blending of fabric, paper, and embellishment.

Beryl's keen eye for design, her ability to integrate so many elements into a unified, beautiful piece of artwork, and her mastery of several disciplines are rarely paralleled. The results are symphonic, each embellishment and stitch like an orchestral instrument, contributing to the beauty of the entire piece without calling too much attention to itself.

Much of the enjoyment of studying Beryl's work is trying to figure out exactly how she accomplished a piece of art. What surprises most people is that many of the tools and embellishments she uses can be found at your local craft store. If you are like me, you may have whizzed right by many of these seemingly ordinary items thinking that you've seen those same supplies used time and time again. But Beryl views many of these same tools and embellishments with fresh eyes, constantly imagining how she can adapt them to suit her work.

It is with great pleasure that I welcome you to the innovative world of mixed-media artist Beryl Taylor. In this book you'll be introduced to her methods of design, learn to experiment with various media, and perhaps try your hand at creating one of the mixed-media projects presented here. Beryl is a gem of an artist and person—her vision and artistic soul are sure to delight and inspire.

Patricia Chatham Bolton
Editor-in-Chief
QUILTING ARTS MAGAZINE®
CLOTH PAPER SCISSORS®

Beginnings
CHAPTER I

THE EARLY YEARS

I became an artist in spite of—not because of—my surroundings. I was born in Rotherham, England, in 1950, and my family moved to Manchester when I was very young. Like many families, mine was affected by the hardships of World War II and my parents worked long hours to make ends meet, leaving little time or money for excursions to museums and other artistic venues. Still, I showed artistic talent in elementary school and began studying at the Manchester High School of Art at age 13.

By then it was the Swinging Sixties, the days of psychedelia and the start of "designer" clothing. Without the money to buy these fashions, I taught myself to sew and eventually became quite a good dressmaker. Yet on finishing high school I took a job in a bank and then as a nurse to help support my family. Marriage and children came next, and after 12 years of homemaking I discovered "creative embroidery."

Creative embroidery

Suddenly, after all these years, it all came together: the love and knowledge of art, the ability to sew, the desire to be the best that I could be, and what do you know, a City & Guilds course that was to change my life forever. All these circumstances led me to become an artist.

City & Guilds

What did being a carpenter or a bricklayer have to do with art? That was the question that immediately ran through my head when someone suggested that I take a City & Guilds course. In the early 1990s, City & Guilds was synonymous with vocational qualifications for artisans rather than artists. It wasn't until it was explained that they also provided non-vocational courses in art and design and, of particular interest to me, in creative embroidery, that I realized this would be a way not only to improve my basic sewing skills but also to teach me how to channel those sewing skills

into works of art. Understanding this process is extremely important, but it is only a supplement to and not a substitute for one's own creativity.

In those days the course was in two parts and each part was structured over a two-year period. Part I covered basic stitch designs, the history of embroidery, introduction to research into different types of embroidery, creation of prepared working design boards, and the initiation into other forms of art that would become integral parts of our ultimate goal. This would include papermaking, distressing fabrics, tearing fabrics and papers, and many other like processes; there were so many things to learn! There were also many things to see, because we didn't just sit in a classroom; we were out "in the field" at galleries, museums, exhibitions, and other centers of learning. Not only were we exposed to what the general public sees but we were also allowed access to archives that are never open to public view yet are so important to study from the artist's perspective. These City & Guilds activities suddenly took over my life and became the greatest learning experience imaginable. Whenever the opportunity arose, outside of my normal working hours, I would participate in one of these activities, much to the annoyance of my husband and

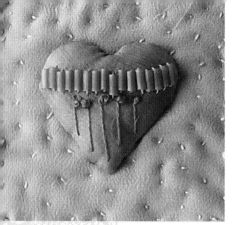
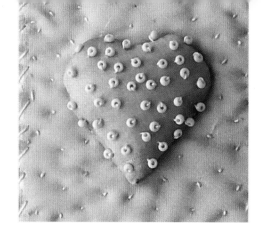
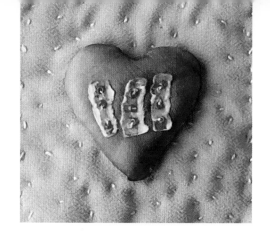

son who both felt neglected, but to the great delight of my daughter who was starting to develop her own interest in art and sewing and who, when not involved in her gymnastics activities, used to accompany me on these excursions.

Part II built upon Part I and focused on experimentation. How do you describe "experimentation"? For me, it was like being released, and the person who freed me was my tutor, Joan Archer. She gave me the freedom to try things but in a very structured way. I couldn't have had a better mentor than Joan. She is a longtime member of the Embroiderer's Guild and the Textile Society, she has been a verifier for the City & Guilds Institute, and in the year 2000 she was awarded an MBE (Member of the British Empire) by Her Majesty the Queen of England for services to further education; I would say that she has the utmost respect of everyone in the field of embroidery. With her vast experience as a teacher, she was keenly aware of the need for the student to instigate the experiment and would coax and cajole us until we came up with the right formula for making the experiment a success. They say that "success breeds success," and certainly when you have had a successful experiment you are inspired to do more. Generally my experiments were successful, but Joan would never allow me to become complacent and would always encourage me to achieve that little bit extra.

A textile group is born

So there I was: a graduate from the City & Guilds course and still trying to juggle my art and my work as a nurse. I was full of ideas that I wanted to express through my art, but without the class-room. I had a need to continue along the road on which Joan Archer had placed me and I now needed a vehicle in which to present my ideas. Should I join one of the groups of textile artists that had formed in the Manchester-Cheshire area or should I try to continue to work on my own?

At that time, it was important for me to have the interaction with like-minded artists that can spark inspiration and cultivate ideas. Some of my fellow graduates felt the same way, and we decided to take the rather adventurous step of forming our own new group of textile artists that we called Threadmill. Within the group we set goals for ourselves and had regular meetings to discuss our work and share ideas, but most notably we started to exhibit our work as a group. To do this we had to produce work based on the theme of the particular exhibition. This provided me with a solid basis for the future and taught me how to produce work to the specifications set by organizers, within a given timeframe. However, after working in this way for a few years, I began to feel that the "themed" work was actually limiting the progress of my art.

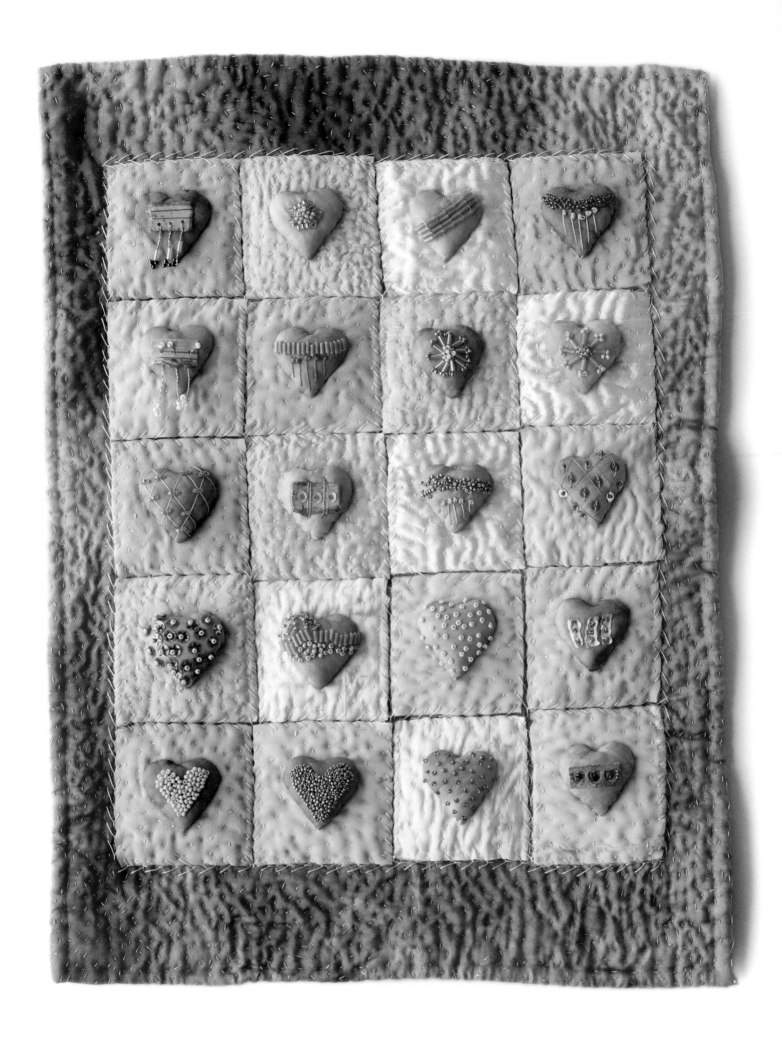

New lands, new discoveries

It's funny how fate often lends a hand. One day my husband asked if I would like to live in New York; he had seen a position advertised and was tempted to take it. I had always wanted to go to America and agreed without hesitation. The wheels were set in motion, and before long we were making a weekend visit to Long Island to find a home. The move allowed me to retire from nursing as well as make a graceful exit from Threadmill. In addition, hardship of all hardships, I could spend as much time as I wished doing my artwork—obviously after completing the normal everyday chores of the homemaker.

But things don't always work out as you expect. That first year-and-a-half on Long Island was like the TV show "Fawlty Towers." So many of our friends came to visit it seemed like we never left Manchester, and the "hotel" was never closed. Don't misunderstand me, I love to see my friends and have visitors, but entertaining them left me little or no time to devote to my work. Then, after 18 months we moved to New Jersey where my husband was setting up a new office. We bought a new house that had ample room in a very nice setting, conveniently situated. What more inspiration could I possibly need to get started on my work in earnest?

I have been working as a full-time artist now for more than three years. The works you see here are some of the fruits of my most enjoyable labors. And now I want to share the joy of creating with you.

GETTING STARTED

Some people feel a bit intimidated when they see my work because it's so detailed. But it's really just a matter of having an idea and then playing with paper, fabric, supplies, and techniques until you get the look you want. In this book I'll share with you what inspires me as an artist and walk you through the steps of how I create a finished project. I'll demystify design principles and impart to you some of my favorite materials, many of which you can easily find at your local craft store. We'll play with these materials in mini-experiments and then make smaller projects, such as artist trading cards, so you get comfortable incorporating the techniques into a design. When you're feeling confident, in chapters IV and V I'll show you how to develop your ideas further into more intricate and detailed wall hangings and books. Are you ready? We're about to have a lot of fun!

Sources of inspiration

We're all inspired by different things, but what gets me going is the beauty of form, color, and texture that I see all around me. In particular, I am inspired when I travel to new places or see books, new or old, which are full of exciting and romantic photographs of far-off places or have beautiful flowing calligraphy. Architecture, costume, antiquities, animals, flowers, writing, and poetry all feed the source of my energy. Once my imagination is sparked, I keep it fired by listening to my favorite music, and no one inspires me more than Andrea Boccelli.

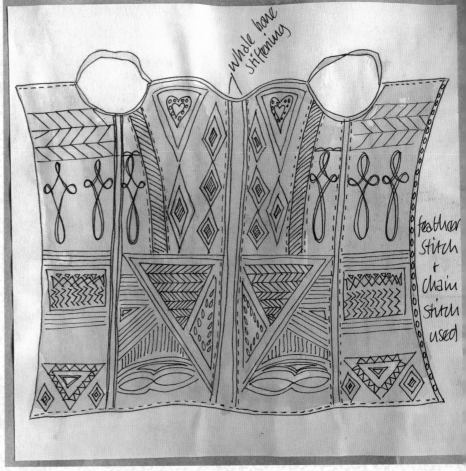

One of my favorite sources of inspiration is the Medieval period. I love the architecture, the colors, and the motifs that were widely used during that time. Anything Gothic attracts my attention immediately. I think gargoyles are items of great beauty and, although grotesque by comparison, I see them in the same light as angels, which I believe have had a tremendous effect on my life and my work. Fleur-de-lis and hearts are constant motifs in my designs as well. I admit I'm a bit obsessive about collecting images, rubber stamps, and embellishments that have the fleur-de-lis design.

Once you begin to focus on finding inspiration around you, ideas will come, and you will need a way to keep track of them. I suggest you buy one of the very compact digital cameras that are easily carried in your pocket. You will find that wherever you are, something will catch your eye and spark an idea or creative vision. With your camera, you can quickly record it. Later, the photograph will remind you of the idea and away you go.

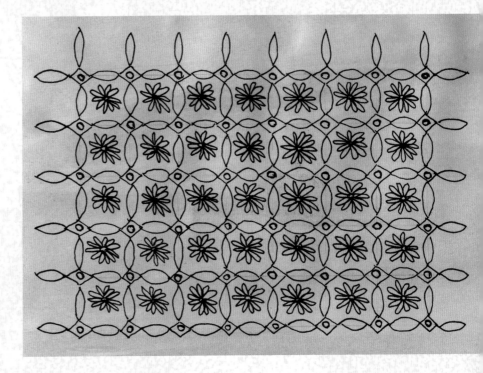

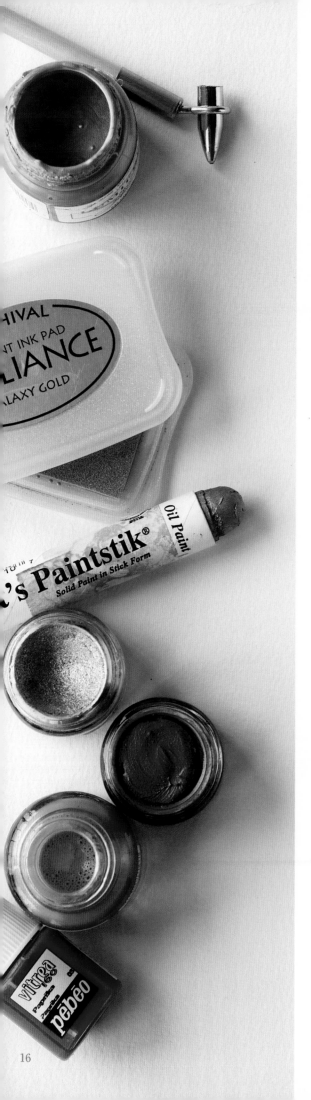

MATERIALS & TOOLS

When I first started on my journey, I used to travel light; my tools were needle, thread, machine, and fabrics. As the journey became longer, the load became heavier, and as I added to and developed the media in which I worked, the tools became more varied. Some have expanded from the typical artist's gear to include synthetics, plastics, burning tools, and cutting devices. From a creative point of view, you should not be afraid to try anything that you believe will produce and enhance the quality of the finished piece. However, you should always be sure to take any necessary safety precautions when dealing with equipment and materials that could be dangerous if not used appropriately. This includes heat guns, irons, heavy punches, and materials that could become toxic when subjected to heat or used in association with other materials. Whenever possible I use non-toxic materials; when that is not possible, I always wear safety clothing, a mask, and goggles, and I work in a well-ventilated area.

Below is a list of materials and tools that I use in most of my work:

▪ DIP PEN A dip pen is a metal nib attached to a penholder. It doesn't hold ink like a fountain pen, and therefore you have to keep dipping the pen into the ink to write and draw. I also use a dip pen with bleach, drawing onto inked paper.

▪ PAPERS I use papers for backgrounds, edges, centerpieces, embellishments—in fact, just about anywhere I choose. I color them with paints, inks, and dyes. I bleach them, stitch them, cut them, fold them, and curl them. Some of my favorites are:

Lokta paper: This Nepalese paper has a natural look about it. It is long-lasting and durable, yet folds easily.

Mulberry paper: This paper has lots of texture and its edges feather easily when wet.

Japanese tissue: This paper is quite strong. It comes in different patterns and colors.

▪ VELVET Velvet is a pile fabric that is luxurious to the touch. Cotton velvet has a strength and stability that is ideal for bleaching, whereas silk velvet is more slippery to handle but feels more sumptuous and can be stamped. I like to use both. I also use synthetic, stretchy panné velvet. The only drawback is that it has to be put into an embroidery hoop to be worked on properly.

▪ HOT WATER-SOLUBLE FABRIC This fine polyvinyl fabric feels like very thin plastic. It needs to be doubled in an embroidery hoop to be stitched on, but is ideal for creating lacy patterns. When immersed in hot water, the background polyvinyl disappears leaving just the lacy embroidery.

Mixed-Media Explorations

- **METALLIC RUB-ONS** These wax-based polishes are housed in small pots and come in a variety of colors. You apply them with your finger and they are great for accenting raised areas. I use Treasure Gold metallic wax finish.

- **HAND AND MACHINE THREADS** Threads are used for stitching on paper, fabric, and metal. My favorite machine threads include Isacord, a polyester thread that runs smoothly through the machine and won't break easily. It has a matte finish and comes in large spools of 1,000 meters (about 1,100 yards) each. I also use DMC and Madeira metallic threads. I recommend metallics with caution as they can be temperamental and break easily.

  The choice for hand threads is vast, from DMC Embroidery Floss to silk threads of various weights and colors. I often get specialty threads from the Internet.

- **CORDS** I use Bourdon cord, but you can use a very fine piping cord and dye it yourself. Bourdon cord is a continuously wrapped cord that gives off a wonderful sheen. I like to couch this onto a design with a fine thread.

- **STAMPS** I use both rubber stamps and polymer stamps. Polymer stamps are transparent, making it easier to position your stamp image where you want it. Whether using rubber or polymer stamps, I look for simple designs that are deeply etched. Many stamps have fine, intricate details, but the images don't reproduce well when using thick media.

- **GESSO** Gesso is a thick (white or black) chalky mixture that can be painted onto paper or fabric to provide a rough-textured surface. I usually coat it onto cotton muslin with a spatula.

- **SHIVA PAINTSTIKS®** Shiva Paintstiks are sticks of oil paint in solid form that look like large crayons. The outer coating must be peeled off before each use because the sticks self-seal after 24 hours. I like to use them on fine silk, employing a relief-rubbing technique using a rubber stamp.

- **MODEL MAGIC** Model Magic is a form of spongy, very light, non-toxic modeling clay that air-dries after 24 hours. You do not have to add water, it does not leave a mess, and it is easily painted. I usually use this in thick layers or pieces, because the thin layers have a tendency to crack and break. Model Magic is very good for impressing into rubber stamps, but you need to dust the stamps first with talcum powder or even baking flour to prevent the clay from sticking to the stamp.

- **PAINTS** Acrylic paint is a fast-drying synthetic paint that dries to a shiny finish. I do use some fabric paint, but not often, as I have had good results using acrylic paint on fabric. It can be applied in thick coats to produce a textured surface or diluted with water (my preference) to obtain a finer consistency.

Watercolor is a transparent paint that lets the surface of the papers shine through the colors. It is good for washes using a large brush. I also like to use it in smaller, concentrated areas using a smaller brush.

Watercolor Crayons are crayons whose "coloring" turns into paint when water is applied. I like these crayons because they come in vibrant colors and are easy to use.

Glass Paint is a solvent-based paint that creates a stained-glass effect on glass and acetate. I have used it on metal, too. I paint it on metal with a brush and when dry, I sand it with a fine-grade sandpaper to obtain a distressed look. The most widely available brand of glass paint is Pebeo Vitrea.

Pebeo Gel is a transparent, non-yellowing gel medium. I mix this with acrylic paints to produce a thick, self-colored textured surface on fabric. It is safe to heat with a heat gun. I also paint it as a base on Kunin felt so embossing powders will adhere more readily.

■ INKS Pigment inks typically come in vibrant colors. They are quite thick in consistency and dry slowly; for this reason they are excellent for use with embossing powders and rubberstamping.

Dye-based inks are fade-resistant and often water-resistant. I like them because they are fast-drying. I use these for rubberstamping.

Gold ink is one of my favorites. I apply it with a fine brush to highlight my work. The metal particles usually migrate to the bottom of the bottle and need to be frequently agitated, but it is well worth the effort.

Writing ink is good for "painting" paper. This is the same kind of ink made for use with a dip pen, but you apply it to your paper with a brush for this use. Then patterns can be created on the paper with bleach applied with a pen.

■ PELLON® This is a non-woven polyester backing. I use heavyweight Pellon to create a support for unstable textiles that require more body, and a firm, smooth application, such as silk, gauze, and chiffon. It can also be used on its own as a canvas for painting. I usually obtain it from a yard-goods store in the craft section.

■ WONDERUNDER® WonderUnder is a fusible web product with a paper backing (often called "release paper"). It must be ironed to adhere it to fabric. I use it for creating interlays. It can also be painted and covered with foils. I always save the release paper and use it to protect my iron from paints and other surface applications.

■ KUNIN FELT Kunin felt is a blend of acrylic and polyester fibers that melt when heated. I cover it with embossing powder and impress it with rubber stamps. I like it because melting the edges with heat produces a very effective aged or worn appearance.

SYNTHETIC FABRICS I prefer the cheap, stretchy, velvety types of these man-made fabrics. I like to work them in an embroidery hoop, etch designs into them with a soldering iron, and I often fuse multiple layers together.

CHIFFON SCARVES These gauzy, sheer scarves are transparent and come in a variety of colors. Like synthetic fabrics, they contract and melt when subjected to heat. They can also be etched with a soldering iron. I use these scarves in my layering processes, but also to retain other materials in a "sandwich" by bonding two layers together with WonderUnder and then machine-stitching through the entire layered construction.

METAL SHIM These thin sheets of metal can be found in most craft stores, are usually sold in a roll, and come in brass, copper, and aluminum. I use the lightweight grade, cutting it into shapes that I then machine-stitch into my work.

XPANDAPRINT This is a thick, creamy medium that can be applied with a brush, roller, or sponge. It expands when heated and it is non-toxic. It comes in black or white, can be painted on before or after heating, and is soft enough to stitch through; this is ideal for my work. I usually use a heat gun to expand it, but if you do not have a heat gun, you can use a hot iron from underneath. It's perfect for use with rubber stamps.

FRIENDLY PLASTIC These flat sticks of metallic-colored plastic become soft when heated. In this condition they can be impressed with rubber stamps. This product is non-toxic.

TYVEK® Tyvek is made from high-density polyethylene fibers and has the characteristics of paper, film, and fabric. When heated it shrinks and distorts, and I use the resulting effect quite a lot in my work. I usually use a heat gun on Tyvek, but you can also use a hair dryer or an iron.

PVA GLUE I use PVA glue for most projects and find its versatility very useful. It goes on white and dries transparent. The drawback is that it is water-soluble. On fabrics I use Sobo Glue® because it doesn't penetrate the fabric.

SEWING MACHINE I have a Bernina Virtuosa 155 that is ideal for my work. I bought it for its free-motion features, its automatic embroidery stitches, and its reliability—all of which are second to none. I mainly use two types of feet, the zigzag foot and the free-hand embroidery or quilting foot. If you are going to be doing any machine work, I recommend getting a machine that has these features.

TOUR
DU
MONDE

◼ MISCELLANEOUS MATERIALS

Watercolor Paper I use Fabriano 140-lb. I like this for its strength, thickness, and stitchability.

Silk Fabric I use habotai, 8mm or 10mm, 60 - 80 gram-weight that I dye myself.

Dyes I use both Deka Silk dyes, which come in a liquid form, and Procion dyes that come in powder form.

Needles I use a variety of needles in my work, depending on the materials I am working with. For machine-stitching thicker fabrics, paper, and metal shim I use 90 - 100 size. Paper and metal will dull the needle faster than fabric, so I keep several on hand so I can change the needle frequently. For machine-stitching finer fabrics I use 70 - 80 size. For hand-beading I use fine beading needles. For hand-stitching finer fabrics I use small needles with small eyes, and for heavier fabrics I use a tapestry needle that has a larger eye.

Batting I use polyester batting for deeper quilted effects but I use felt to back finer quilt projects. When stitching into polyester batting, you achieve greater "depth" because the thickness of the polyester is greatly reduced by the stitch. Felt is much thinner, so stitching does not produce great depth.

I have given you a long list of suggested materials, but unless you want to break the bank, you probably can't buy them all at once. An invaluable lesson that I learned from my own frugal beginnings was to use—and use creatively—what's on hand. So perhaps if you don't have everything on my list, get a few of the things that you find most intriguing, add them to your stash of favorite embellishments and tools, and then we can start playing.

Experimenting

❧ CHAPTER II ❧

It's a good idea to spend time experimenting with new techniques and materials and then to log your experiences in a journal. You never know if you can use them in a finished piece. My first attempts in experimentation involved fabric and paper and produced samples of stitching, burning, and layering. Other manipulative techniques I used involved bleaching on paper and stitching on hot and cold water-soluble fabrics. Having successfully completed the City & Guilds course, I continued to experiment with new materials and techniques that I had not previously encountered, some of which are illustrated here. Try the exercises below to get started on your own experiments.

BLEACHING PAPER

1. Paint handmade Nepalese paper with black writing ink.

2. Using a dip pen and bleach, draw a design onto the inked paper.

3. Hand-stitch a triangular-shaped paper centerpiece and frame it in strips of fabric.

4. Incorporate gold cord and stitching in gold thread to accentuate the bleached pattern.

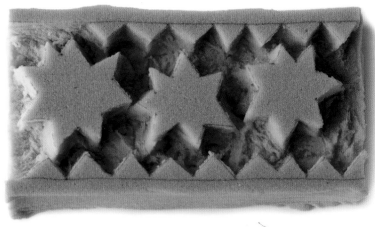

BLEACHING VELVET

1. Create a stamp for the background pattern by cutting the image into a piece of sponge; the denser the sponge, the better.

2. Take the stamp and dip it in bleach, just enough to wet the sponge—not dripping wet.

3. Impress the image onto a piece of black cotton velvet and leave it to dry.

4. Next, make the red centerpiece stars by cutting a potato in half and carving a star image into the face of the potato to make a raised stamp.

5. Melt red crayons down to form a liquid and dip the potato stamp into the liquid.

6. Stamp onto the bleached velvet making a wax impression and leave it to cool.

7. Apply gold rub-ons to the surface of the waxed impression.

8. Decorate the background with embroidery using small seed stitches over the main area and long stitches around each main star.

9. Cut small triangles of gold paper and stitch them into the corners of the main stars with beads.

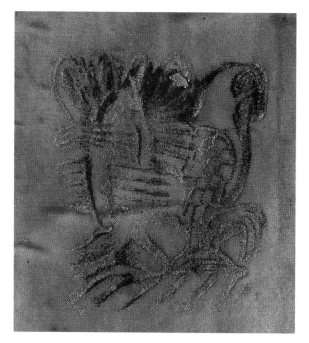

Working with SHIVA ARTIST PAINTSTIKS®

1. Lay a piece of fine silk over a rubber stamp.

2. Holding it firmly in place, rub the top surface with a dark-colored Shiva Paintstik followed by a gold Shiva Paintstik. *(above).*

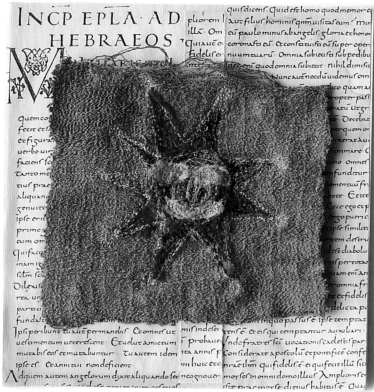

Stitching on HOT WATER-SOLUBLE FABRIC

1. Stretch the water-soluble fabric into an embroidery hoop. I recommend using two layers of fabric to make it stronger and therefore easier to stitch on.

2. Machine-stitch in a grid pattern (the lines must cross to form an interconnecting web to prevent the stitching from unraveling when the water-soluble fabric vanishes).

3. Lay cords over the grid lines and stitch them in place using a zigzag stitch.

4. Cut small pieces of fabric and machine-stitch them into some of the squares formed by the grid pattern.

5. In some squares, zigzag stitch over the threads at the corners; leave some of the squares unadorned.

6. When you have completed your design, remove the hoop and immerse the work in hot water. The water-soluble fabric will dissolve, leaving the finished piece. Let dry. *(see photos at left and above)*

Working with MODEL MAGIC® BY CRAYOLA®

1. Roll out the Model Magic to the desired thickness and cut to the desired size.

2. Press the piece firmly onto a rubber stamp and then gently peel the stamp away. When using regular rubber stamps, sprinkle a small amount of powder on the stamp first as this will help the Model Magic peel off more easily. Alternatively, you can use polymer stamps as the Model Magic won't stick to them.

3. After you've peeled off the Model Magic from the stamp, leave the resulting Model Magic tiles on a flat surface overnight to dry.

4. When dry and stiff, paint with watercolor paints, and when the paint is dry, rub over raised areas with metallic rub-ons for a more textured look.

Working with WATER-SOLUBLE PAPER BY SOLVY®

1. Tear some water-soluble paper into small squares.

2. Stack 3 of the squares on top of a rubber stamp.

3. Apply a small amount of water to your fingers and press the papers into the stamp to create a mold.

4. Leave to dry overnight and, when dry, peel the mold off the stamp.

5. Paint the sample with the desired base color, allow it to dry, and then rub with metallic rub-ons.

6. Mount the samples by machine-stitching onto gesso-painted fabric.

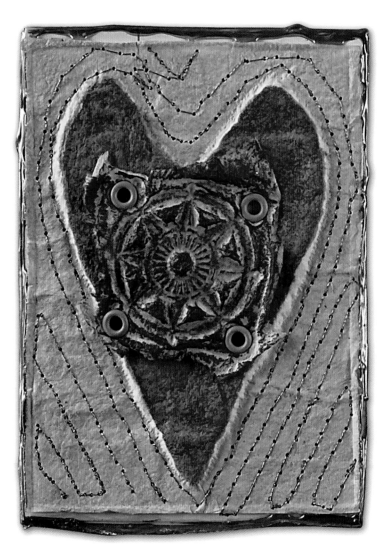

Mixed-Media Explorations

5. Peel off the WonderUnder release paper and iron on a layer of craft foil, again using a warm iron and parchment paper.

6. Decorate the piece with hand stitching.

Sandwiching (below)

1. For sandwiching and trapping embellishments and thread snippets, take a piece of cotton fabric and arrange tiny snippets of colored yarns, colored threads, and gold thread onto the surface of the cotton.

2. Iron on a layer of WonderUnder (face down) using a warm iron.

3. Peel off the WonderUnder release paper (the backing) and iron on a layer of chiffon, again using a warm iron and making sure to use the release paper or another piece of parchment paper to protect your iron from the fusible glue.

4. Decorate with French knots and fly stitching.

EMBEDDING & SANDWICHING

Embedding (above)

1. Take a piece of Pellon and paint it with diluted acrylic paint.

2. Lay strips of torn silk and some shisha mirrors on the Pellon and iron a layer of WonderUnder on top. Use a warm iron and place parchment paper between the iron and the WonderUnder to protect the iron.

3. Peel off the WonderUnder release paper and iron on a layer of chiffon using a warm iron and parchment paper.

4. Iron a further layer of WonderUnder on top, adopting the same technique.

Working with
PELLON® INTERFACING

1. Take a piece of Pellon (I used a 3" x 3" square) and paint it with diluted acrylic paint.

2. When dry, stamp an image onto the Pellon 4 times, using gold pigment ink, once in each quarter of the square.

3. Cut out the 4 images and glue them to a piece of velvet.

4. Using gold thread, hand-stitch gold cord around the perimeter and between the squares.

Etching into VELVET

1. Paint a layer of WonderUnder lightly with diluted acrylic paint.

2. When dry, iron the WonderUnder onto a piece of synthetic velvet using a warm iron and parchment or release paper as previously described. (The velvet can be the stretchy, panné velvet type.)

3. Peel off the WonderUnder release paper and iron on a layer of gold foil, again using a warm iron and parchment paper.

4. Put the layered velvet into an embroidery hoop and tighten securely.

5. Use a wood-burning tool and a variety of tips to burn different patterns into the velvet.

6. Apply strips of assorted synthetic fabrics to the velvet and attach them with the burning tool. Decorate with hand stitching.

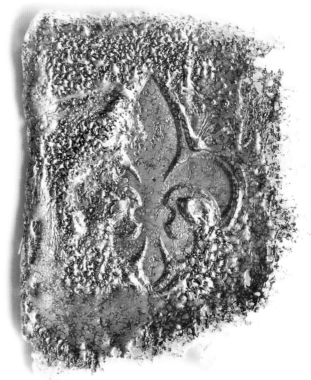

UTEE OR ULTRA-THICK EMBOSSING ENAMEL™
on fabric

1. Take pieces of cotton velvet or Kunin felt and paint them with either Pebeo gel or acrylic opaque gel (both of which are very thick).

2. Before the gel dries, sprinkle with embossing enamel powder and heat with a heat gun.

3. While the first layer of embossing powder is still hot, apply a second layer and heat again.

4. Prepare a rubber stamp by applying pigment ink to the stamp. Apply a third layer of embossing powder to your piece, heat this layer, and press the inked stamp into the hot surface.

5. Allow to cool before removing the stamp.

XPANDAPRINT

1. Machine-stitch strips of watercolor paper together with gold thread.

2. Iron on a layer of WonderUnder face down using a warm iron.

3. Peel off the WonderUnder release paper and iron on a layer of chiffon, again using a warm iron and release paper.

4. Take a large stencil and brush Xpandaprint through the pattern onto the chiffon.

5. Remove the stencil and, using a heat gun, heat the Xpandaprint carefully to raise the surface. Do not overheat.

6. Allow the Xpandaprint to cool and then paint the raised pattern and finish with metallic rub-ons.

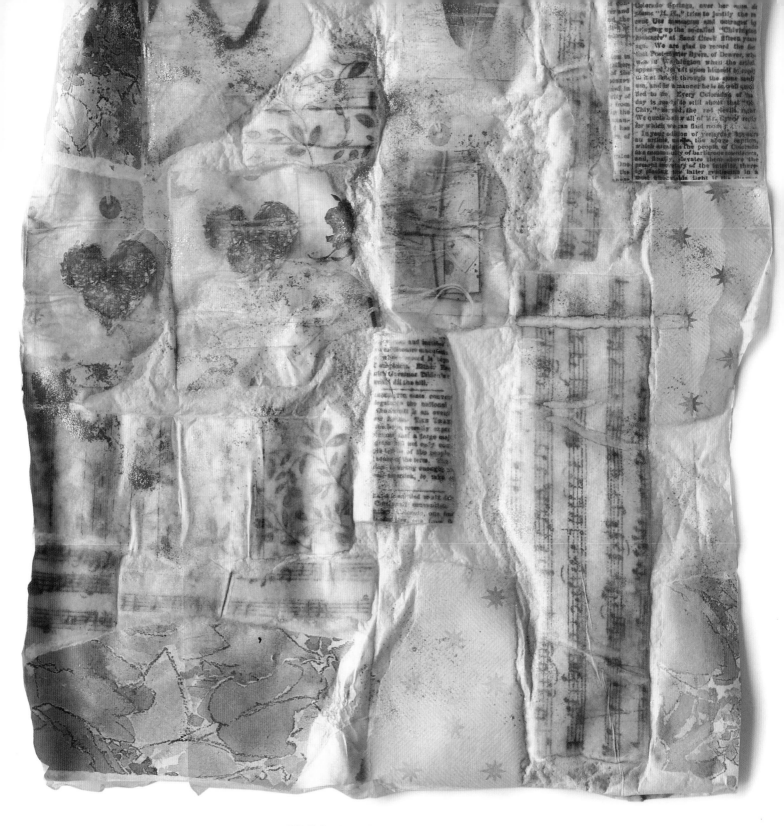

TYVEK® PAPER

1. Take a piece of Tyvek (I used a Tyvek envelope for the sample), cut to size, and cover with PVA glue.

2. Tear copyright-free photocopied images, gift wrap, and wallpaper into squares and rectangles and place them onto the glued paper, leaving spaces between.

3. Apply a layer of PVA glue over the top.

4. Tear craft tissue into strips and place the strips onto the glued paper.

5. Wash the whole area of the finished paper with diluted acrylic paints of desired color.

Mixed-Media Explorations

STITCHING METAL

1. Hammer the head of a large screw into the back of a fine metal shim. (You will want to do this on a cutting mat or similar surface to protect your worktable.) This will produce the pattern of the screw head on the front of the shim.

2. Cut out the desired shape and paint the front with Pebeo glass paint.

3. When dry, sand gently with a fine sandpaper.

4. Lay the metal shape onto a piece of velvet that has been fused to black felt and, using a needle made for stitching through leather, machine-stitch around the edges.

5. Embellish with colored cane, shaped wires (a round-nose pliers works great for this), and beads. The small sample here has been machine-stitched onto a recycled tea bag background that is backed with felt.

FRIENDLY PLASTIC

1. Take a strip of Friendly Plastic and cut to desired length.

2. Heat with a heat gun until soft and press a rubber stamp into the hot surface; wait for a few seconds before removing the stamp.

3. If you wish to make holes in the plastic, do this before it hardens.

4. I find the natural colors of the Friendly Plastic to be too bright and prefer to tone them down with metallic rub-ons.

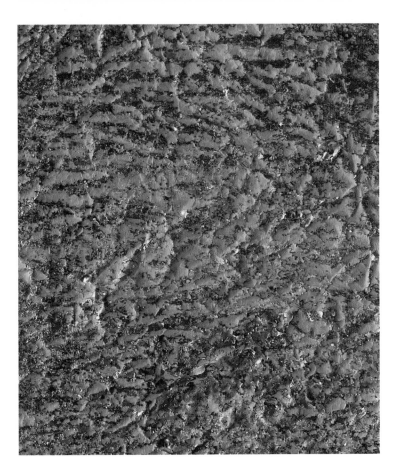

FOILED BROWN PAPER

1. Scrunch up brown paper (I used a supermarket bag for the sample) and flatten it out with your hand.

2. Iron on a layer of painted WonderUnder, using a warm iron.

3. Peel off the WonderUnder release paper and iron on a layer of foil, again using a warm iron and the release paper.

WALLPAPER

1. Glue strips of wallpaper of various widths onto a piece of felt.

2. When dry, glue small strips of craft tissue over the top and paint with diluted acrylic paints.

3. When dry, rubberstamp with a script image.

4. Iron on thin strips of WonderUnder using a warm iron.

5. Peel off the WonderUnder release paper and iron on a layer of foil shiny side up, again using a warm iron and release paper.

WALLPAPER & PLASTER of PARIS

1. Glue strips of wallpaper of various widths onto a piece of felt and allow to dry.

2. When dry, glue small strips of craft tissue over the top and paint with diluted acrylic paints.

3. When the paint is dry, randomly apply a thin layer of plaster of Paris and allow to dry.

4. When dry, iron on thin strips of WonderUnder using a warm iron.

5. Peel off the WonderUnder release paper and iron on a layer of foil, again using a warm iron and the release paper to protect your iron.

FABRIC PAPER

1. Take a piece of open-weave muslin and paint it all over with diluted PVA or white glue.

2. Embed wrapping paper, images, and text into the glue layer, leaving spaces between.

3. Apply another coat of diluted PVA or white glue over the top. Embed craft tissue into this glue layer.

4. While the glue is still wet, paint on dyes using a sponge applicator.

FLY
STITCH
each stitch
looks like a
y' and is
repeated from
left to right

SIX CLASSIC HAND STITCHES

I use the following six stitches frequently and interchangeably in my work. As you'll see in my stitch book, you can make many creative variations with just one stitch. The following illustrations will walk you through the basic steps for each stitch.

Fly stitch

FLY STITCH

Bring the thread through at the top left. Hold it down with the left thumb and insert the needle to the right on the same level, a little distance from where the thread first emerged. Take a small stitch downwards to the center with the thread below the needle. Pull through and insert the needle below the thread, as shown, to hold it in place. Bring the needle up again in position to work the next stitch.

Mixed-Media Explorations

SATIN
STITCH
IS A STRAIGHT
FLAT STITCH
WHICH CAN
BE WORKED
IN ANY
DIRECTION

SATIN STITCH

Work straight stitches close together across the shape, as shown. Take care to keep the edge even, and if you are following an outline marked on the fabric, take your stitches to the outside of the line so that the marked line does not show.

Satin stitch

HERRING-
BONE
STITCH
A BORDER
STITCH WHICH
IS USED TO
MAKE A CROSSED
ZIGZAG LINE

HERRINGBONE STITCH

To practice the herringbone stitch draw three parallel lines horizontally on your fabric about ¼" apart. For our purposes here, we will call the middle line the seam.

1. Come up at A a scant ¼" below the seam. Go down at B.

2. Take a small stitch from B to C above the seam.

3. Go down at D and then take a small stitch to the left from D to E.

4. Repeat.

Once you've mastered the basic form, you can get creative with spacing and stitch length. For left-handers, follow the same instructions except move the needle from right to left.

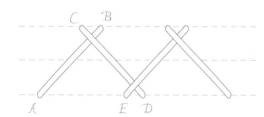

Herringbone stitch

CHAIN STITCH

The chain stitch is remarkably flexible—whether woven, twisted, zigzagged, whipped, or opened, it can be stitched in a variety of ways. Stitched with one or two strands of cotton floss, it can be used to embroider names, dates, or interlocking circles. While not ideal for seam work, the chain stitch can be used if you zigzag or undulate it on either side of the seam.

1. Bring the needle up at A, down at B, and up again at C. Make sure the needle comes out at C over the thread.

2. Repeat step 1 (inserting needle at D) for each stitch.

For left-handers: Follow the same instructions except reverse the positions of A and B so you begin on the right and move to the left.

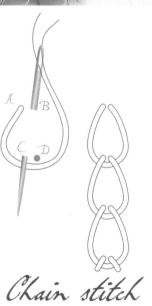

Chain stitch

FRENCH KNOTS
when the thread has been twisted once or twice round the needle

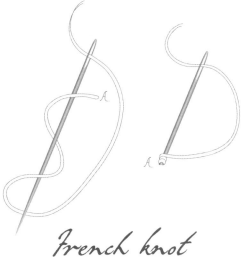

French knot

FRENCH KNOT

1. To make a French knot, simply bring your thread or yarn up from the back of the work in the place where you would like the knot to appear.

2. Wrap your thread around the needle 2 times.

3. Keeping the thread or yarn taut, insert your needle back into the work immediately next to where the thread first emerged.

4. Pull the thread through to the back of the work, and your knot is complete. If your knot is not as large as you would like, do not wrap it around the needle more than 2 times. Instead, use a thicker thread.

BLANKET STITCH

1. To begin the blanket stitch, find your baseline. In the illustration, the baseline is the dashed line at the bottom of the stitches.

2. Come up at A.

3. Insert the needle into the fabric at B, and bring it back out at C. Your working thread must be under the needle, so that it catches. The resulting stitch should resemble a backward L.

If you are left-handed the resulting stitch will look like a standard L. Generally, right-handed stitching begins on the left end of a seam, and left-handed stitching begins on the right end of a seam.

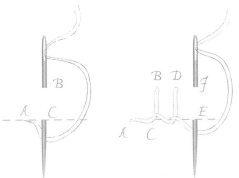

Blanket stitch

Elements of Design

CHAPTER III

When an idea strikes like a sledgehammer, you can't wait to get started on the work itself. But where do you begin? I don't believe you necessarily have to follow a rigid process to produce a piece of art. We are individuals and, as such, we each have our own way of working. It's important to follow your own path because that is when you produce your best work. Some artists instantly have a vision of the end product and are able to work toward that end. Others start with the germ of an idea but quite often find that as the piece develops the original idea is overtaken by the natural flow of their creativity. Personally, I think that I fall into the latter category. When I formulate an idea for a piece of work, I like to start by making sketches. Then with the aid of photocopies, rubber stamps, and other accessories I've collected along the way, what may have started out as a bit of a jumble slowly develops into the framework for the finished product.

Quite often this process will take place instinctively, but sometimes I develop design boards. These could be equated to the storyboards used by film directors. Design boards help me to choose the most appropriate materials, develop particular techniques to be used, and provide me with direction for the most effective use of those materials and techniques.

In the following pages I will share some of my artwork and the techniques used to create them in hopes that you will be inspired to experiment and play and create your own wonderful pieces.

Mixed-Media Explorations

DESIGN TIPS & TRICKS

All artists have their own way of working and being creative; they do not necessarily stick to strict processes. Every piece that I produce is different from the last, and the way I produce the piece is usually different as well. Having said that, and having analyzed how I approach a new piece of work, I would say that, generally, I follow a process similar to that outlined below.

Method

My normal "modus operandi" is to work on a small scale; my larger pieces, such as wall hangings, are produced by incorporating several smaller pieces into a larger piece. This often produces a work of art that has a symmetrical pattern based on the recurring theme of the motif found on the smaller pieces.

Design steps

1. I first determine the motif that will be the basic theme for the piece.

2. Next, I select the basic color scheme, which usually stems from the choice of motif. Do I need a vibrant color that will draw attention to the whole piece or do I need a more subtle color that will allow the detail to stand out?

3. Third, I choose the media I will use to create the piece, e.g. paper(s), fabric(s), metal, clay, etc.

4. The last step is to determine the "depth" of the piece. In my work I usually use at least two layers, and often more. At this stage, I lay out the materials on my worktop in much the same way that a painter would lay out the basic colors on his palette. I start to construct the piece in loose form to see if it can realistically be put together in the manner in which I have envisioned it. By doing this I can see right away whether or not an element or color is going to work in the final piece, and make changes if necessary. Sometimes it is more difficult to determine which of the several possible elements or colors will best enhance the piece. In my earlier days, this process was usually supplemented by producing a "design board," but I find that after several years of experience, I am now able to get straight into producing the piece.

Production tips

- I find it important to have all of my tools readily available when I'm working because I never really know what techniques I will adopt until I actually start working on the piece.

- I usually produce the background first. I use felt or batting underneath most pieces to give them support and to make them easier to work on.

- Having formed the background, I build up the depth of the piece by layering. At this stage I have already decided which part of the piece will be revealed at each layer and I then detail and embellish each layer individually. When all the layers are completed I overlay them and connect them by machine and/or hand stitching.

- Finally, I produce the main motif or centerpiece. I hand-stitch this to the background, and any final embellishments such as beading, cording, etc. are also hand-stitched.

A CLOSER LOOK

Some people say my work looks difficult to do. In reality, most of my pieces are actually a series of small projects that are then combined. It's the layering and attention to detail that makes the finished work look complex.

In this piece, entitled "A is for Always," I started by choosing a pastel palette. I then created and embellished several smaller pieces and appliquéd them onto a larger background. To better understand the sequence of how I did this, look at the black-and-white illustration at right. You'll notice how the smaller elements are finished first, then added to the larger base. To help create cohesion, I repeated several motifs and design elements in a few places, such as the cluster of three mother-of-pearl buttons, the heart motifs, and the flowers.

1 A strip of water-soluble paper was stamped and colored, then five small snippets of sheer organza were equally spaced on top. Tags embellished with brads, beads, and stars were then placed on top of each of the five organza pieces. When this embellished strip was completed, it was then hand- and machine-stitched to the larger base.

2 Small flower shapes and circles were cut from paper, colored, and layered. A small piece of sheer novelty fabric was stitched in this section on the base, then on top. Each of these two decorative elements was secured to the piece with a small, white bead. *(right)*

3 The letter "A" was drawn on hand-dyed habotai silk that had been fused to a felt base. The "A" was then machine-stitched along the edges with gold thread, cut out from the silk panel, and machine-stitched to the fabric paper. The edges of the fabric paper were gilded, then this completed piece was hand-stitched to the larger base. *(left)*

4. A strip of embossed decorative wallpaper was painted with brown watercolor paint and when dry, the embossed text was rubbed with metallic gold. The strip was then machine-stitched to the base with gold thread. *(left)*

5. A fleur-de-lis motif was created with Model Magic and a rubber stamp, and when dry, colored in pinks and golds. It was then glued to a rectangular base of fabric paper. Three small mother-of-pearl buttons were hand-stitched on top, then this embellished piece was appliquéd to the larger base. *(left)*

6. A strip of paper was colored, rubberstamped, torn in a rectangular shape, and glued to the base. *(above)*

7. A strip of fabric paper was colored in blue, then cut to create a jagged, triangular edge along the bottom. The edges were then colored in gold, machine-stitched with gold thread, and stitched to the larger base. *(above)*

8. Five tiny tags were each embellished with a small metal charm, then attached to the base with a pink eyelet. *(right)*

9. Modeling paste was spread over a rectangular piece of fabric. Two holes were cut in the center of the fabric and metallic frames attached to these openings with brads. The fabric panel was then stitched to the background piece and metal hearts were placed in the holes and hand-stitched in place. *(left)*

10 A small strip of colored paper was embellished with five squares of paper that were each stitched to the base with a combination of a gold seed bead and a bugle bead. Once embellished with the beads, the piece was glued to the larger base. *(above)*

11 A small piece of paper was rubberstamped, colored, and embellished with three small, floral designs that had been made from water-soluble paper impressed into a rubber stamp. The designs were painted with watercolor paint and attached to the paper with a small, gold seed bead. *(top right)*

12 A heart was colored onto a base of fabric paper. The outline of the heart was machine-stitched with gold thread, then machine-stitched diagonally in both directions to create grids. Small, gold seed beads were then stitched in the center of each of the grids. After three small mother-of-pearl buttons were stitched along the bottom, this piece was hand-stitched to the base. *(right)*

13 A rubber stamp with a spiral sun image was used to impress water-soluble paper. Once the water-soluble paper was dry, it was colored magenta and gilded. Then a window design was rubberstamped onto colored paper. The inside of the window shape was cut out and the window then glued on top of the spiral sun shape. A piece of sheer and glittery novelty fabric was cut and machine-stitched over the whole piece. This piece was then machine-stitched with gold thread to the larger base and accented with two gold beads on the upper corners. *(right)*

14 A small rectangular strip of gold paper was punched with a flower-shaped paper punch. A strip of sheer, glittery novelty fabric was placed on top, then the entire piece was machine-stitched to the base. *(left)*

15 Two small charms (one with a heart motif, the other a ribbon motif) were each attached to a piece of 4mm silk ribbon. The silk ribbon was then wrapped around a small tag that had been colored. A small, pink brad was used to attach each of the tags to the larger base. *(right)*

PRACTICING *with* SMALL PROJECTS

I devote most of my time to producing larger pieces and experimenting with new materials and techniques, but there is always an occasion for working on a smaller scale. Whose birthday is it this week? Who has just had a baby? Who has just graduated? And yes, whose team has just won the Super Bowl? All of these occasions can inspire an experiment on card stock. I think of my smaller work as another opportunity to try something new that ultimately can be incorporated into my larger pieces—not to mention the fact that the recipients always love to receive them. Here are some simple experiments on card stock that you might like to try yourself.

GREETING CARDS

Rubberstamped card (opposite, top)

1. Prepare a centerpiece by cutting a square of card stock and rubberstamping it with a large color-block image using different colors of pigment ink.

2. When dry, over-stamp with a diamond image. Allow the image to dry and then paint each diamond with a dot of gold paint and set aside to dry.

3. Take a blank greeting card and color it with pigment inks using a stipple brush and by rubbing the surface of the card with the ink pad; leave to dry.

4. Repeat this process on a narrow strip of card stock. Using gold thread, machine-stitch pocket shapes onto this prepared narrow strip of card stock.

5. Repeat the coloring process on 4 small tags and, once dry, stamp the tags with a script image.

6. Cut out 4 flower shapes from contrasting decorative paper and attach 1 flower to each tag with an eyelet in the center of the flower.

7. Attach a bead to each tag string and place a tag in each pocket.

Fabric paper (opposite, bottom)

1. Cut a piece of fabric paper (see Chapter II for directions on making fabric paper) to the exact size of the greeting card (front and back).

2. Using gold thread, machine-stitch around any motifs in the paper (in the example I free-motion stitched around the flower design). Hand-stitch sequins and beads in the middle of the motifs.

3. Cut out another rectangle of fabric paper for use as the centerpiece of the card. In the center of the rectangle, place a circle of scrapbook paper with script.

4. Cut out a motif such as a flower shape in contrasting paper and place it over the circle. Hand-stitch a sequin and a bead in the center of the flower, being sure to catch all layers. Glue the centerpiece onto the card.

5. Cut small strips of decorative paper and glue them around the edges of the centerpiece.

materials

- Rubber stamps: diamond-shaped image, script, and a color-block image
- Decorative paper
- Pigment ink
- 4 small tags
- Ink pad
- Stipple brush
- Eyelets
- String

materials

- Scrapbook paper with script design
- Decorative paper
- Sequins
- Beads
- Gold thread

materials 1

- Decorative paper
- Blank greeting card
- Friendly Plastic
- Watercolor paints
- Watercolor paper
- Gesso
- Heat gun
- Script stamp
- Gold wire
- Gold beads
- Sewing machine
- Gold thread

materials 2

- A page from an old book
- 7 buttons
- Glue
- Thread
- Gold wire (coiled)

materials 3

- Photocopy of an antique button card
- Blank greeting card
- Thread
- Mother-of-pearl buttons (# to match photocopied image)
- Felt

1. Friendly Plastic *(opposite, top)*

1. Take a piece of decorative paper and cut a strip 1 ¼" x 4 ¼". Glue this strip to the front of a blank greeting card.

2. Take a piece of watercolor paper 2 ¾" x 2 ¼" and apply a wash with watercolor paint. When dry, dab with gesso and leave again to dry.

3. When the gesso is dry, stamp it with a script design and glue it to the greeting card, partially covering the decorative paper strip. To add more texture, machine-stitch with metallic thread on an edge of one of the papers as I have here.

4. Take a piece of Friendly Plastic, heat it with a heat gun until soft, and imprint it with a rubber stamp. Make 4 holes along the bottom edge while the plastic is still soft.

5. Take 4 short lengths of gold wire, each about 1 ¼", thread a gold bead at one end, and twist the wire around to secure the bead. Thread the other end of the wire through the hole in the Friendly Plastic and retain by threading a gold bead onto the other end, as before.

2. Buttons on squares *(opposite, bottom left)*

1. Tear a page from an old book and paint it with watercolor paint. When dry, tear it into ¾" squares.

2. Glue approximately 7 squares on top of one another to form 1 layered square. Repeat until you have 4 layered squares.

3. Sew a button on top of each layered square and glue the squares to a piece of decorative paper.

4. Take 3 pieces of fine gold wire, cut to desired length, and create coils. Hand-stitch the coils onto the decorative paper.

5. Machine-stitch your completed centerpiece onto a blank greeting card.

3. Mother-of-pearl buttons *(opposite, bottom right)*

1. Photocopy an antique button card and hand-stitch mother-of-pearl buttons over the original button images.

2. Lay the photocopy on a piece of felt and machine-stitch around the edge, attaching it to a blank greeting card.

3. Hand-stitch 2 additional buttons directly onto the greeting card to finalize your pattern.

Mixed-Media Explorations

POSTCARDS

Card stock postcard (top left)

1. Cut a piece of card stock to postcard size.

2. Using a stipple brush, paint the card with a desired color, applying greater saturation at the edges.

3. Tear a piece of scrapbook paper printed with a diamond design and glue it to the left-hand side of the postcard.

4. Rubberstamp the card with text and images in contrasting colors. Finally, glue sequins to the already applied diamond design.

Fabric paper postcard (left)

1. Cut 2 pieces of fabric paper to postcard size and back each piece with cotton fabric. These 2 pieces will form the finished card, one being a front piece and the other being the back.

2. Rubberstamp the front piece randomly with desired images.

3. Rubberstamp half a clock face on vellum paper and glue it to the card front.

4. Cut out half a clock face from a scrapbook image and glue it to the card front below the stamped clock image.

5. Rubberstamp a separate piece of card stock with an image of camera film. Cut around the image and apply it to the card front, framing the clock faces. Machine-stitch in position.

6. With gold thread, stitch the back piece to the front piece using an automatic machine blanket stitch.

materials

CARD STOCK POSTCARD

- Stipple brush
- Paint
- Scrapbook paper with a diamond design
- Rubber stamps
- Sequins

materials

FABRIC PAPER POSTCARD

- Fabric paper
- Cotton fabric
- Scrapbook paper with a clock image
- Rubber stamp with a film image
- Sewing machine
- Vellum paper
- Glue
- Gold thread

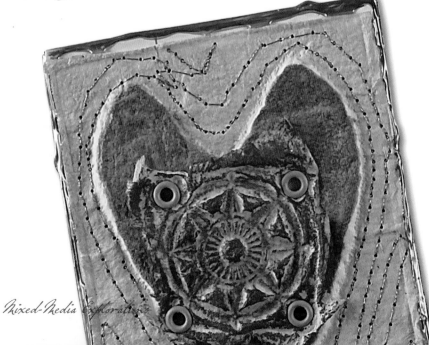

ATCS

What on earth is an ATC? That was my reaction when I was first asked to produce one. I am sure that most American readers will know that this is an Artist Trading Card, but having spent most of my time in the U.K., this was a new concept to me. Artist Trading Cards (ATCs) are miniature works of art that artists swap with each other, as the name suggests. Unlike my regular business card, ATCs not only identify my work, they also enable me to build up a very nice collection of art of varying styles from fellow artists. ATCs are also a wonderful way to try out a technique without a large investment of time and materials, and they are so much fun to make and share, they are addictive.

You can create ATCs with any materials (fabric, paper, metal, etc.) and embellish them as you like. Typically, they measure 2½" x 3½"; artists back them with card stock and sign and date the card, often adding contact information such as an email or web address. You can make each one a piece unto itself or create a short series (in which case artists usually number them).

Note: *Almost any material you would use for quilting or mixed-media art can be incorporated into an ATC. What makes it an ATC are the dimensions and your imagination.*

The following are a few samples of ATCs that I have recently exchanged.

materials

FOR ATC BACKS
- 2½" x 3½" piece of card stock
- 2½" x 3½" piece of felt

Mixed-Media Explorations

Paper Heart ATC

1. Tear rectangles of water-soluble paper (Paper-Solvy™) and layer them onto the heart image on the stamp. I usually use 3 layers. The first layer should barely be dampened, just wet enough to allow it to adhere to the stamp. The following 2 layers should be fairly moist to allow you to push them into the stamp. Allow to dry overnight.

2. Take the dried paper off of the stamp and paint it with desired color. If using watercolors, add as little water as possible to the paint.

3. Construct the centerpiece motif in the same manner but, when dry, finish with metallic rub-ons rather than paint.

4. Attach the centerpiece to the card with eyelets placed at each of its corners.

5. Machine-stitch the card front to the backing with gold thread.

6. Cover the backing with paper and edge with Krylon gold pen.

materials

- Water-soluble paper
- Heart-shaped rubber stamp
- Water
- Paints
- Eyelets
- Gold thread
- Krylon gold pen

Mixed-Media Explorations

Star AK

1. Take 3 strips of silk, each ½" x ¾", lay them onto a felt background, and machine-stitch them together with the overlapping edges.

2. Decorate the card using an automatic heart-design stitch on the sewing machine.

3. To create the centerpiece, place a piece of rayon or silk velvet into an embroidery hoop and tighten. Lay a stencil with the desired design over the fabric and apply Xpandaprint to the stencil.

4. Carefully remove the stencil and use a heat gun to heat the Xpandaprint until it becomes puffy. Allow this to cool and dry and then paint it with an acrylic metallic gold paint.

5. Allow the paint to dry and then paint it again, this time with a patina antiquing solution.

6. Once the patina is dry, dab the image with metal leaf adhesive size and apply gold leaf.

7. Machine-stitch the centerpiece to the card.

8. Cut a piece of card stock to size for the backing and machine-stitch in place with gold thread. Cover the backing with silk and decorate the edges with Krylon gold pen or acrylic paint.

- Silk
- Felt
- Sewing machine
- Rayon or silk velvet
- Embroidery hoop
- Stencil of choice (in the example I used a star)
- Xpandaprint
- Heat gun
- Metallic gold paint
- Patina antiquing solution
- Krylon gold pen or gold acrylic paint

materials

- Silk
- Felt
- Gold thread
- Sewing machine
- Friendly plastic
- Heat gun
- Heart-shaped rubber stamp
- Metallic rub-ons
- Beads
- Gold thread
- Krylon gold pen or acrylic paint

Friendly Plastic Heart ATC

1. Use a rectangle of silk with felt backing as the basic card.

2. Use a smaller piece of felt as a background to the centerpiece and overlay it with 3 strips of silk. Use gold thread and machine-stitch through the strips of silk to attach the background to the basic card.

3. Cut a piece of Friendly Plastic, heat it with a heat gun until soft, and then impress it with a heart-shaped rubber stamp for about 5 seconds. Remove the stamp and make holes in each corner of the plastic with an awl, or other pointed object, while it is still soft.

4. When the image has cooled, treat it with metallic rub-on to tone down the color. Hand-stitch the plastic centerpiece to the background through the pre-drilled holes at each corner, attaching a single bead each time.

5. Cut a piece of card stock to size for the backing and machine-stitch the card to the backing with gold thread. Cover the backing with silk and decorate the edges with Krylon gold pen or gold acrylic paint.

Clown AK

1. Attach a rectangle of printed fabric with a diamond motif to a piece of felt to make the basic card.

2. Stitch gold beads onto the center of each diamond on one half of the card.

3. Randomly paint a piece of watercolor paper with watercolor paint and some gesso. (I use Fabriano 140-lb. watercolor paper.) When dry, tear down the edge that will be in the center of the card.

4. Rubberstamp the card with the clown and diamond images using black pigment ink. Place the decorated paper onto the card and machine-stitch around the edges with gold thread.

5. Cut a piece of card stock to size for the backing and machine-stitch the card to the backing with gold thread. Cover the backing with silk and decorate with Krylon gold pen or gold acrylic paint.

materials

- Fabric with a diamond motif
- Gold beads
- Watercolor paper
- Watercolor paints
- Gesso
- Clown stamp
- Diamond stamp
- Gold thread
- Black pigment ink
- Krylon gold pen or gold acrylic paint

Fiber art

CHAPTER IV

s I explained in Chapter I, my larger pieces, such as wall hangings, are produced by incorporating several smaller pieces into the main large piece. This was certainly true of my earlier works and is well-illustrated in the production of one of my earliest pieces, a corset. The idea of creating my own corset came about after studying early costume design. Initially, I planned to do a full, three-dimensional design, and so I produced a design board—something I strongly encourage you to do to develop your designs. You will see that the board contains designs and motifs on a small scale that ultimately translate to the larger piece. Actually, working on the board led me to change my thoughts on the piece, and the original 3-D design evolved into a wall hanging.

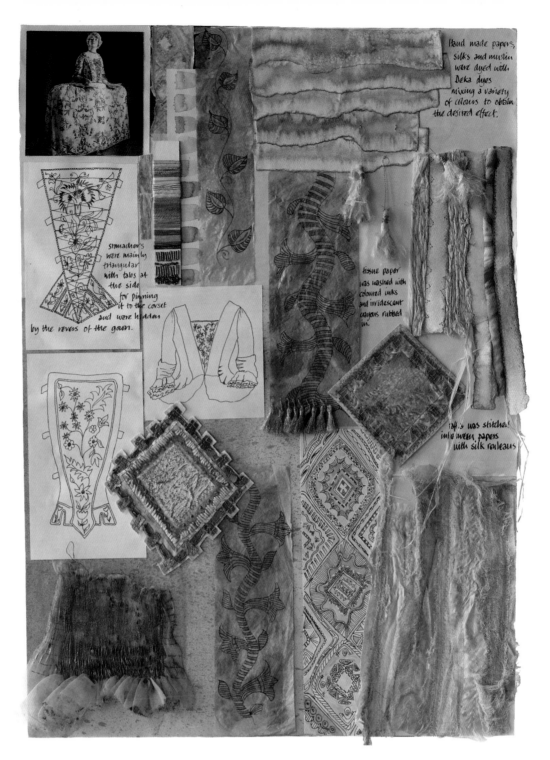

Hand made papers,
silks and muslin
were dyed with
Deka dyes
mixing a variety
of colours to obtain
the desired effect.

stomachers
were mainly
triangular
with tabs at
the side
for pinning
it to the corset
and were hidden
by the revers of the gown.

tissue paper
was washed with
coloured inks
and iridescent
crayons rubbed
in.

raffia was stitched
into woven papers
with silk rouleaus

CORSET

Design board

The original concept was inspired by the idea of a Renaissance stomacher. From that I made pen-and-ink sketches of what was going to be my own design. I kept a sketchbook and produced color schemes and experimental samples using fabrics of various types (such as silk and muslin), papers of differing weights, and combinations of fabrics and papers. It was the latter that made me move toward making a wall hanging. By stitching raffia in conjunction with strips of watercolor paper and tubes of padded silk, I was attempting to replicate the effect of boning that you see in corsets. I found the texture and feel so exciting that I decided to produce the wall hanging with that effect as the main background; the detailing samples became the center panel of the hanging.

Wall Hanging

The center panel of the hanging was
created by placing pink cotton over a layer
of heavyweight Pellon (for support).
Diamond-shaped layers of handmade paper
were machine-stitched in place and their
edges emphasized by building up triangles
of silk machine-stitched in place, layers of
hand-couched bourdon cord, hand-stitched
bugle beading, and different types of hand
stitching and automatic machine stitching.
Strips of silk muslin and thin ribbon were then
hand-dyed and stitched around the edges of the
panel, and left to hang in varying lengths from
the bottom edge of the panel.

The side panels (main background) were constructed
from strips of dyed watercolor paper and alternating
lengths of raffia and tubes of silk padded with batting,
all machine-stitched together.

The hanging device is a dowel wrapped with strips of muslin
that are held in place with cord.

Corset

Having developed the wall hanging from my original desire to produce a 3-D corset, I found myself, some years later, looking at my early piece and deciding that I would develop the theme by creating a full corset front panel.

The background of the panel is made from the brown paper used for grocery bags. This was crayoned and painted, covered with a layer of craft tissue, and glued to the surface. Then the tissue was painted with dyes.

The center panel is made from two diamond-shaped pieces of silk, hand- and machine-stitched to the background and padded from the back through a small opening left in the stitching. Gold beads were hand-stitched to the diamonds with gold thread. Strips of paper were hand-stitched with decorative stitching around the outline of the diamond, and pieces of cane couched down with thread at the perimeter of the paper strips. The spaces between the diamonds and the edges of the panel are decorated with hand stitching and small squares of gold paper hand-stitched to the background. The center panel is separated from the side panels by vertical lines of gold beads, hand-stitched in gold thread.

The side panels are made from strips of colored paper that were decorated with rectangles of metal shim hand-stitched to the paper. Between the rectangular strips of metal shim, additional layers of square-shaped paper and layers of fabric were all hand-stitched and embellished with gold beads. The fully decorated strips were then stitched in rows, vertically, to the background. These strips alternate with rows of large fly stitches.

The cup shape was formed with a brown paper background using a bra as a mold. Strips of colored watercolor paper were hand-stitched across the background using a large fly stitch.

The bottom of the corset is edged with a strip of watercolor paper that was decorated with calligraphy, accordion-folded, and machine-stitched to the background.

"Timely Gems" • 10½" x 9¾"

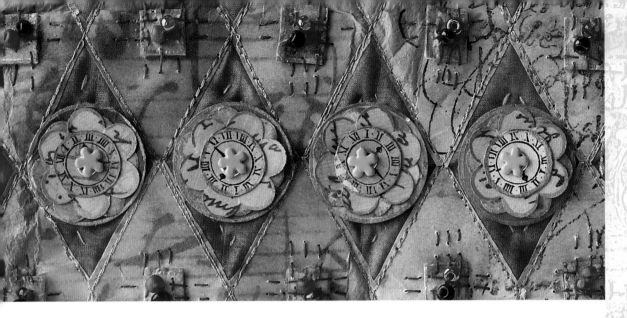

MOUNTING, HANGING,  FRAMING

When I produce smaller pieces of work for wall mounting, I do not always frame them. However, if I don't frame them I like to mount them on mat board because I believe this makes the work more presentable.

With the larger wall hangings the hanging device can vary, but I find that I usually create loops at the head of the hanging through which I insert a wooden pole or dowel. I then attach a cord at each end and hang it from a hook on the wall. I often wrap the pole in fabric or paint it, and sometimes I add finials to each end. You can design and embellish all of this "hardware," as well as the hanging devices, to become integral parts of the piece.

When I decide that a piece should be framed, I usually opt for a simple design and material so that the eye is not diverted from the real content of the work. I almost always use professionally made shadowbox frames because my work has so much depth. On occasion I have mounted 3-D pieces in Plexiglas box frames so that the art can be viewed from all angles.

GALLERY

'Timely Gems'

The simple shape of a diamond inspired this piece. The main background consists of two layers of my fabric-paper process, one piece slightly larger than the other. The first, larger layer was machine-embroidered with gold thread around the edges. The smaller layer was decoratively hand-stitched to the first layer in two vertical lines and the piece then edged with gold leaf pen. The focal decorative layer (the diamonds) was made of fabric paper machine-stitched to a layer of felt-backed silk. The individual diamonds were machine-stitched, and alternate diamonds cut out of the paper to expose the colorful silk underneath. Once the fabric paper was machine-stitched to the silk layer, the resulting sandwich was hand-stitched to the main background with simple straight stitches. The exposed silk diamonds were embellished with circles, flowers, and clock faces of decorative paper, all held together with either an orange or pink brad in a star shape. The paper diamonds were embellished with small squares of paper edged in gold leaf, beading, and stitching.

"Come In" • 10½" x 4"

'Come In'

The inspiration for this piece (above and right)
came from doorways, the main piece being a layered
doorway that, when opened, allows us to see beyond.
As in many of my larger pieces, this is made up of
interconnected smaller pieces. The main media are
watercolor paper and silk. I have also incorporated
photo-transferred images, strips of beading and
eyelets, and tiny hanging tags.

"Saffron Hues" • *14½" x 11¾"*

'Saffron Hues'

The inspiration for this piece came from an old Indian painting that I photo-transferred onto silk as the centerpiece. Made mainly of silk, the background is machine-stitched and the foreground hand-stitched and quilted. Embellishments include beads, wire, handmade papers, and a tassel.

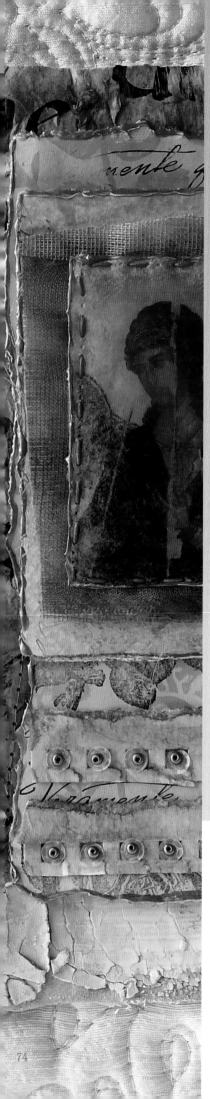

"By Your Side" • 12" x 7½"

Betsy Taylor 05

'By Your Side'

The inspiration for this piece was an image of an angel that I had had for a long time
and had never previously incorporated in my work. The image was photo-transferred onto
silk to make the centerpiece. This piece is made mainly of silk and the background is
machine-quilted. The foreground is made of layers of different papers incorporating
decoration, calligraphy, and applied gesso. Beads and sequins embellish the piece.

Mixed-Media Explorations

"Hearts and Leaves" • *20" x 4½"*

'Hearts and Leaves'

The title explains the inspiration for this piece. The main medium is fabric paper; the piece was constructed from several small elements machine-stitched and glued to a fabric-paper background. The images are mostly rubberstamped. The rose image was rubberstamped onto paper and also onto shrink plastic which starts out at the original paper size but, when subjected to heat, shrinks to a considerably smaller scale. Embellishments include beads, gold wire, metal leaf motifs, and sequins.

Beryl Taylor 2000

'Domino Gloria'

The inspiration for this piece came from a Medieval tile I discovered while carrying out research. The main medium is fabric paper, the background is made from 16 individual squares in a tile pattern decorated with text, and the foreground is a circular design incorporating flower heads overlaid on the background "tiles." The flower heads are decorated with gold leaf and embellished with red silk tassels.

"Phulkari Peacock" •
12" x 12"

'PHULKARI PEACOCK'

The inspiration for this piece came from the Indian Peacock. The background is a square of handmade paper. The piece itself was constructed from the centerpiece which is a machine-embroidered peacock surrounded by random hand stitching around which strips of different colored silks were machine- and hand-stitched. These strips of silk were then decorated with paper, beads, wire, and machine embroidery. The four outer corners were finished with squares of handmade paper and embellished with beads.

"Castles in the Air" •
14¾" x 15½"

'CASTLES IN THE AIR'

The inspiration for this piece came from Medieval architecture. The piece consists of three velvet panels that were cut in the shape of towers. The upper edges are crenellated and decorated with paper, cane, beads, and squares of fabric. The center panel is decorated with an arch of gold embroidered paper, edged with cane. The upper sections of the two outer panels were decorated with arched window panels of paper edged with cane; the lower sections with squares of paper embellished with beads and larger panels of paper hand-stitched to the velvet.

Now that you've had a chance to see some of my finished pieces, why not try your hand at completing a larger piece? The following art pieces are fairly easy to accomplish, fun to create, and will help you practice working on a larger scale.

tools & materials

- Brush
- Felt
- Gold cord
- Glue
- Knitting needle or skewer
- Machine thread, gold
- Needles for hand-stitching
- Pen
- Polyester filling
- Sepia ink
- Sewing machine
- Silk fabric in 2 contrasting colors
- Small amount of metallic chiffon in different colors
- Scissors
- Tea bags
- Watercolor paper, 140-lb
- 18 sequins
- 18 gold beads

BIRD HANGING

The background

1. Brew some tea and let it steep. Take a piece of watercolor paper and apply a wash of tea water with a brush. Leave it to dry.

2. When dry, use sepia ink to write text, filling the page. Couch around the edge of the background with gold cord.

The centerpiece

1. For the centerpiece, take a rectangular portion of patterned silk and lay it over felt. Sew the silk to the felt by repeating an automatic pattern stitch with your sewing machine until the panel is covered with stitches.

2. Take a piece of silk in a contrasting color and cut 3 bird-shaped motifs from it. Turning under the edges of the cutouts, hand-stitch the bird motifs to the silk panel, leaving a small opening in the stitching of each motif.

3. Take small amounts of polyester filling and, using a knitting needle or skewer, push the filling into the bird shapes through the openings in the stitching; be careful not to overfill. When you are happy with the shape and depth of the motifs, stitch the opening closed.

4. Cut 2 wing-shaped pieces of metallic chiffon in contrasting colors for each motif. Distress the edges of the wings to produce a torn and aged appearance. Apply the wings to the motifs, in 2 layers, couching gold cord around the wing.

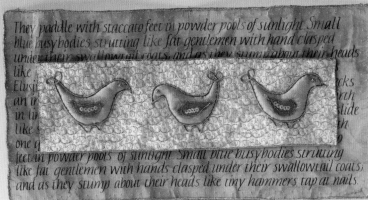

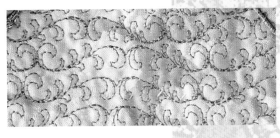

"Bird Hanging" • 6¾" x 13"

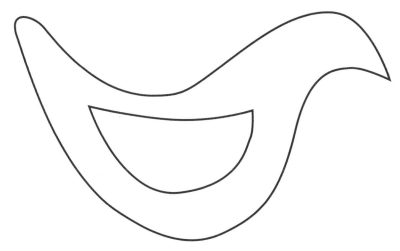

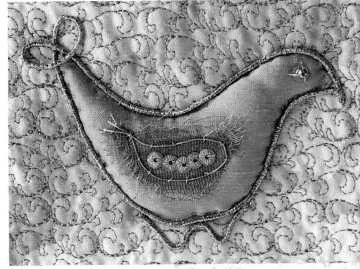

5. Decorate each wing with 5 sequins, each with a gold bead hand-stitched into the center using gold thread. Sew the sequins and beads in a row centered across each wing.

6. Create the eyes for each bird with a sequin and gold bead. Embellish the edges of the motifs with gold cord couched in place; form the tails and feet with loops in the cord. Glue the centerpiece to the background.

Betty Taylor '01

Mixed-Media Explorations

ANGEL HANGING ('HEARTFUL')

The background

1. Take 2 pages from an old book. Crumple the pages, re-flatten, and apply a wash with different colors of watercolor paint. Leave to dry.

2. When dry, rubberstamp script images over the pages.

3. Take a star-shaped stencil and apply Xpandaprint to the stencil. Carefully remove the stencil and heat the Xpandaprint with a heat gun until it puffs up. Paint the star image with gold metallic paint and leave to dry. Repeat the process until all the stars have been made.

4. When dry, paint the star shapes with patina fluid. Allow the fluid to dry and apply gold leaf with gold leaf adhesive.

The angel

The centerpiece angel is built up in four stages: first the body piece, the head and hands, the heart, and finally the wings.

THE BODY & PETTICOAT

1. Trace the head and body (including petticoat) on felt and cut out. This will be the base of your angel to which you will glue the decorative body, head, and wings.

2. Cut the body shape from fabric paper. Cut the petticoat from fabric paper of a contrasting color and glue to the back of the main body.

3. Decorate the body with strips of colored paper that have been rubberstamped with desired images before gluing to the body.

4. In between the strips of decorated paper, hand-stitch gold hearts punched from card stock. Additionally, decorate the lower strip of colored paper with long stitches over the strip and embellish with gold beads.

5. Decorate the lower part of the body with paper squares of a contrasting color rubberstamped with heart images and then glued to the body.

6. Below the hearts, hand-draw a pattern with your drawing pen and finish the bottom of the body with sequins secured in place with gold beads.

7. Decorate the petticoat with strips of colored paper and glue in place. Embellish the first strip of paper with small lengths of cane couched in place with thread. Embellish the lower strip with curls of gold wire couched in place with gold thread. Finally, decorate the lower edge of the petticoat with metal leaf-shaped embellishments.

---

tools & materials

- Beads
- Brushes
- Cane
- Drawing pen
- Felt
- Gold card stock
- Gold cord
- Gold leaf
- Gold leaf adhesive
- Gold metallic paint
- Gold wire
- Glue
- Hand-stitching thread in gold
- Jewelers' round-nosed pliers
- Machine thread in gold
- Fabric paper in different colors
- Metal embellishments, leaf-shaped
- Needles
- Patina fluid
- Pigment ink
- Punch, heart-shaped
- Rubber stamps
- Scissors
- Sequins
- Stencil
- Watercolor paint
- Watercolor paper, 140-lb.
- Xpandaprint

"Heartful" • 15" x 11"

THE HEAD & THE HANDS

1. Cut the shapes from flesh-colored paper. Cut slits in the body for the insertion of the hands and head.

2. Cut the hair shape from a piece of dark-colored paper. Glue the face shape to the hair, paint in the facial features, and finish by applying strips of dark-colored paper to create a fringe.

3. Insert the head into the body slit at the neckline and glue in place. Create the neckline on the dress with gold cord couched in place with gold thread. Insert the hands in the body slits at the wrists and glue in place—but do not glue the actual hands yet, which are left free for the insertion of the heart motif.

THE HEART

1. Cut a heart shape from paper in a color that contrasts with the body. Overlay the heart with a square of contrasting-colored paper and glue in place. Embellish the square with hand-stitched, curled gold wire.

2. Hand-stitch gold cord around the edge of the heart and create a trail at the bottom with gold hearts punched from card stock attached to gold thread.

3. Glue the heart to the front of the body under the hands.

THE WINGS

1. Cut 2 layers from fabric paper for each wing. Cut slits into the wing shape to create feathers and glue the 2 layers together where they attach to the body. *(Wings 1)*

2. Cut 2 further layers for the shorter feathers for each wing and glue them to the larger wing shapes where they attach to the body. *(Wings 2)*

3. Glue all the wing pieces to the back of the body and decorate the wings with the feather shapes and patterns using watercolor and gold paint.

When the angel is assembled with wings, glue the angel to the center of the background.

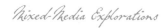

Wings 1

Head

Body

Heart

Hands

Petticoat

Wings 2

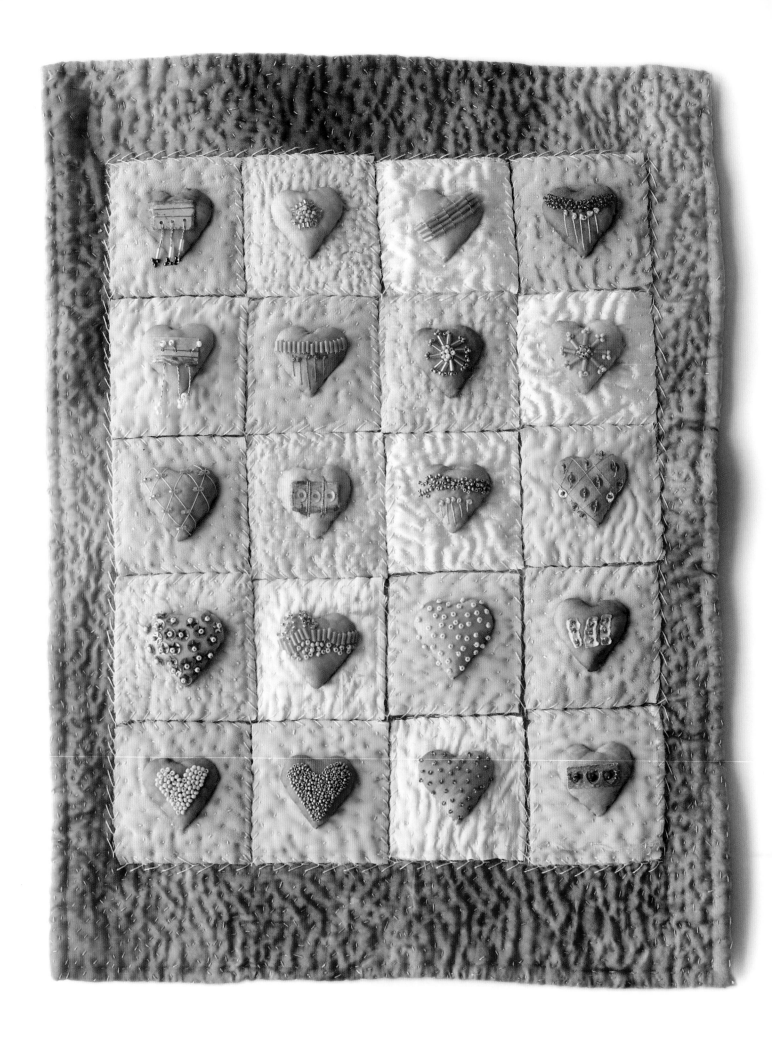

Mixed-Media Explorations

'HEART QUILT'

The background

1. Lay a large piece of silk onto batting to form the background and hand-stitch the whole panel, at random. Turn the outer edges of the silk panel over the batting and stitch down at the back of the piece.

The squares

1. Cut 20 silk squares, 2" x 2", and stitch with a running stitch to felt backing.

The hearts

Make 20 heart motifs as follows:

1. Cut a heart-shaped motif from mat board ($1\frac{1}{8}$" x $1\frac{1}{8}$" overall).

2. Cut thick batting to the same shape.

3. Glue the batting to the mat board. Leave to dry.

4. Cut heart shapes in habotai silk approximately $\frac{1}{2}$" larger all around than the mat board heart.

5. Lay the mat board batting face down onto the silk heart.

6. Pull the edges of silk over the batting and glue to the rear face of the matboard.

7. Decorate hearts with desired embellishments (mine included heart-shaped punch-outs, beads attached to wire strips, sequins, random beads, and French knots).

Finishing

1. Glue the 20 individual hearts to the felt-backed 2" x 2" silk squares.

2. Lay the 2" x 2" squares onto the background and pin in place.

3. Stitch the squares to the background using a decorative fly stitch.

tools & materials

- Batting
- Beads
- Bugle beads (long beads)
- Embroidery thread
- Felt backing
- Fine gold wire
- Glue
- Mat board
- Needles; embroidery
- Needles; beading
- Pliers
- Punch; heart-shape
- Punch; small circle-shape
- Scissors
- Silk; large piece of hand-dyed for background
- Silk; 20 2" x 2" squares of varying color
- Silk; hand-dyed habotai silks for heart motifs
- Sequins
- Watercolor paper

"Heart Quilt" • 15" x 11"

Books & Bindings
CHAPTER V

*a*s I honed my skills and explored new media, I began to look for ways to make my art more intricate and inviting. What better way than with books?

I took traditional bookbinding classes but discovered that classical bookbinding did not allow me the spontaneous changes in direction that I so enjoyed while producing a piece of work. So, I started making my own books, using all sorts of different papers and fabrics and finding different ways to bind them—ways that were not always in keeping with the traditional methods of bookbinding. I created "altered books" and enjoyed exploring them, too. I took other book-making classes, as well. One in particular was with Albie Smith, who introduced me to simpler forms of books made with paper. However, as a child I had always loved the little fabric books that my mother used to buy for me and had always thought that one day I might like to make one of my own. Not only was I able to realize that dream, but have since made many books out of fabric and paper, and books have become one of my favorite art forms.

Why do I love books so much? I love what I find inside, but I also love the feel of them and the sense of anticipation they produce. I like opening a book in expectation, not knowing what is about to be revealed but anticipating new discoveries and hidden secrets. I love to see and feel rich, colored, textured covers with ornate bindings and I love my own books to have all of these things, too. Making books is something that gives me immense pleasure.

BOOK VOCABULARY

AWL: Sharp metal tool used to pierce holes. There are awls specifically designed for fabric and for paper.

BONE FOLDER: A smooth, flat tool used to make clean folds in paper. Once you fold the paper with your hands, a bone folder is rubbed on top of the fold, back and forth, to make the fold crisp.

SIGNATURE: Large sheets of paper or fabric that are folded in half to make a set of four pages.

GUSSET: The "faux" cover that you stitch the signatures to in traditional binding. The gusset is made from the same material as the pages and acts as a lining for the inside front and back covers, hiding any stitching, knots, and other frayed bits resulting from stitching and embellishing the cover.

STYLES & BINDINGS

I make my books in three main styles: accordion, single-page, and traditional. Following are examples of how each binding is done.

valley fold

mountain fold

ACCORDION STYLE

This style includes no formal binding or stitching and thus is very friendly for the budding book artist. It is formed by folding the paper and/or card in a zigzag fashion. I usually use Arches 90-lb. weight watercolor paper that comes in 22" x 30" sheets. I cut this large sheet into long strips, 28" x 6", to yield seven panels, each 4" wide. Using a bone folder, I fold them in a zigzag fashion.

To develop your bookbinding skills while playing with some mixed-media techniques, try starting with the following two projects.

'ANGELS RESIDE HERE'

This accordion-style book is made of watercolor paper painted with watercolor paints and rubberstamped with images. Images were photo-transferred onto silk panels and stitched onto the paper pages. Embellishments include beads, buttons, sequins, and tags.

"Angels Reside Here" • *4" x 6"*

"Vintage Ladies" • 3¼" x 5¼"

This is an accordion-style book made of linen. The front cover page has an opening-door motif with an image hidden within. The inside pages are decorated with images of ladies from old photographs photo-transferred onto silk panels and machine-stitched to the linen. The pages were further embellished with beads and lace.

SINGLE-PAGE STYLE

In this style, a number of single pages are accumulated and inserted one-by-one into the book, sandwiched between a front and a back cover. My binding methods vary for single-page style books. The two styles I use most often are lacing and my version of a Japanese stab binding.

Lacing technique

I sometimes use a "lacing" technique in which eyelets are placed on hinges or tabs that are attached to the pages and are then laced with rope, thread, string, wire, or metal loops.

For single-page style fabric books I make each individual front and back page and then adhere them together to form a two-sided page. For each side, I begin with a piece of hand-dyed habotai silk that I machine-stitch to a felt backing using a running stitch along the edges. Then I decorate the pages as I want with further decorative machine or hand stitching, embellishments, beading, image transfers, charms, or ephemera. Once I have two sides completely designed, I glue the two pieces of felt together with a craft glue (such as Sobo). To reinforce this, I machine-stitch around all of the edges. To hide the raw edges, I then tear habotai silk into a $\frac{3}{4}$" width, fold it lengthwise, and insert the pages into the fold. I secure the fabric with small stab stitches in the same color as the silk strip. I often decorate this binding with beading, picking up a bead on each side as I go. When I've gone around all of the sides, I tie a knot close to a place where I can easily hide it.

"Gothic Book" • 8⅝" x 4"

·SILK BOOK·

As with other single-page style books, each of the pages in this book *(above)* was made individually, decorated front and back, then sandwiched together, with beads, lace, cord or other trim added to the edges. Then the whole book was bound together with cord laced through eyelets. I used a pastel palette of hand-dyed silks and many of my favorite techniques in this book: stamping, layering, and random beading and stitching.

·GOTHIC BOOK·

This singe-page book *(opposite)*, is made of silk with felt padding in the shape of a Gothic window. The cover was decorated with machine stitching, a gold-painted motif, and beaded edges. It has a tab binding made from watercolor paper with metal eyelets and velvet cord ties, beaded at the ends. The pages have rubber-stamped images and photo-transferred images on hand-dyed silk with hand- and machine-stitched decoration.

Making the cover

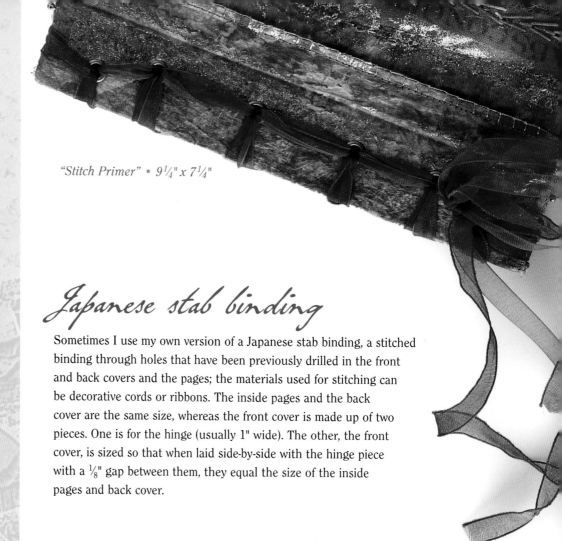

"Stitch Primer" • 9¼" x 7¼"

Japanese stab binding

Sometimes I use my own version of a Japanese stab binding, a stitched binding through holes that have been previously drilled in the front and back covers and the pages; the materials used for stitching can be decorative cords or ribbons. The inside pages and the back cover are the same size, whereas the front cover is made up of two pieces. One is for the hinge (usually 1" wide). The other, the front cover, is sized so that when laid side-by-side with the hinge piece with a ⅛" gap between them, they equal the size of the inside pages and back cover.

An inside page

Cut the board you are using for the cover ⅛" narrower than the inside pages.

Cut the cover board, separating the hinge from the main front cover. Leave a ⅛" gap between these two sections.

HOW TO MAKE BERYL'S JAPANESE STAB BINDING

Follow the stitching sequence below to make my version of a Japanese stab binding.

1. From the back, pass the needle and thread through Hole 3, take them around the spine, and from the back pass the needle and thread back through Hole 3 and then up the front to Hole 4.

2. From the front, pass the needle and thread through Hole 4, go around the spine, and from the front pass the needle and thread back through Hole 4 and then take them up the back to Hole 5.

3. From the back, pass the needle and thread through Hole 5, go around the spine and from the back pass the needle and thread back through Hole 5 and then take them up the front to Hole 6.

4. From the front, pass the needle and thread through Hole 6, go around the spine and from the front pass the needle and thread back through Hole 6, then take them over the top and from the front pass the needle and thread back through Hole 6 and then take them down the back to Hole 5.

5. From the back, pass the needle and thread through Hole 5, take them down the front to Hole 4.

6. From the front, pass the needle and thread through Hole 4, take them down the back to Hole 3.

7. From the back, pass the needle and thread through Hole 3, take them down the front to Hole 2.

8. From the front, pass the needle and thread through Hole 2, go around the spine and from the front pass the needle and thread back through Hole 2 and then take them down the back to Hole 1.

9. From the back, pass the needle and thread through Hole 1, go around the spine and from the back pass the needle and thread back through Hole 1, then take them over the bottom and from the back pass the needle and thread back through Hole 1 and then take them up front to Hole 2.

10. From the front, pass the needle and thread through Hole 2, take them up the back and tie both loose ends of thread together there.

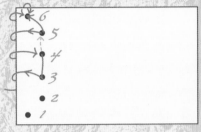

Steps 1 - 4

Steps 5 - 9

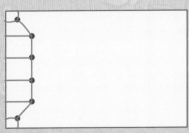

Step 10

"Wedding Book" • *9½" x 12"*

˙WEDDING BOOK˙

My love of romance influenced this wedding album made for a dear friend.
I wanted to create a book that would invite the viewer to lift and discover
endless treasures throughout the book. Mixing fabric and paper is an
effective and fun way to do this. Heart shapes, poetry, silky ribbons, and
amorous words and images all contribute to the romantic theme. The
photograph album was purchased, disassembled for decorating, and then
reassembled and rebound with ribbons.

TRADITIONAL STYLE

The traditional style incorporates signatures (sections of folded paper) that are sewn together at the spine and protected by the cover (front, back, and spine). I always use a pamphlet stitch with the number of holes dictated by the size of the book. (Because my books are typically 6" high or less, I usually use three holes. Larger books, such as the "Checkerboard Book" shown below, typically take five holes.)

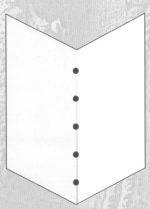

For smaller books, use an awl to make 3 holes along the center fold of each signature.

For larger books, use an awl to make 5 holes along the center fold of each signature.

"Checkerboard Book" • 10" x 8¾"

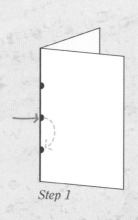

Step 1

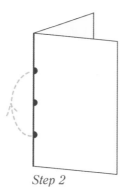

Step 2

Step 3

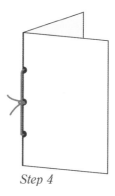

Step 4

Pamphlet stitch

1. The pamphlet stitch starts at the middle hole. You start at the back and bring your stitch up through the hole to the front, then down into the bottom hole.

2. You then take the stitch up the back all the way to the top hole, and bring the thread up through to the front.

3. Finally, come back down through the middle hole. This way, the thread ends up in the back and when you tie a knot with your loose ends, the knot will be hidden.

4. To make the stitching more secure, tie the knot around that bit of long thread that shot up from the bottom to the top. (See step 4 above.)

I usually space the three holes according to the size of the page, starting with the middle one. The middle hole is placed halfway down the page, equidistant from the top and bottom edges. The other two holes are placed 1" in from the top and bottom edges, respectively.

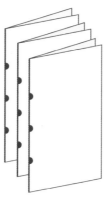
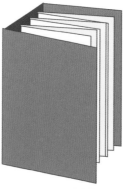

When I create my books I stitch each signature individually to a "gusset" (a lining that is made of the same paper as the pages) that is then glued to the inside front and backs of the book. This gusset also hides any knots, edges, and stitching from the front and back covers.

I use an awl to make the holes in the signatures and gusset and stitch with a strong linen thread. Using a large-hole needle allows the thread to pass through easily.

ʿMEDIEVAL BOOKʾ

The cover of this Medieval hand book is made of stamped, painted, and burned Tyvek, adorned with Xpandaprint stars, beads, and sequins, and has hand and machine stitching on the spine. The individual pages are decorated with Gothic imagery such as birds, arched windows, roses, medallions, and text. All are high-lighted with gold paint, beads, and stitches.

"Medieval Book" • 4" x 5 ½"

ALLYSON'S BIRTHDAY BOOK

This is a traditional book made of water-color paper. The cover is made of mat board covered with fabric and papers that are hand- and machine-stitched with a beaded-circle motif. The signatures are covered with rubber-stamped images and the edges are painted with gold paint. Silk ties with beads and tags hang from the pages.

"Allyson's Birthday Book" • 3½" x 3½"

Mixed-Media Explorations

"Wallpaper Book" • *6¾" x 6⅛"*

˙WALLPAPER BOOK˙

This is a small, traditional book made of watercolor paper. The cover is made of torn strips of wallpaper glued to a felt backing. Layers of gift wrap and pages of text were sandwiched in a layer of tissue and then covered with a thin coating of plaster of Paris and added to the cover. The plaster was painted with diluted acrylic paint and strips of WonderUnder were ironed onto the painted surface. Gold foil was ironed onto the WonderUnder and leaf motifs were painted onto the surface using Xpandaprint and a stencil. The cover was further embellished with machine and hand stitching.

"Fleur-de-lis" • 6¾" x 8"

˙FLEUR-DE-LIS BOOK˙

This is a traditional book made of cotton and painted with gesso. The cover has
a large fleur-de-lis formed with Xpandaprint, floral images formed in water-soluble
paper, and strips of watercolor paper. It was further embellished with hand
stitching and beads. The pages are decorated with different patterns of fleur-de-lis
machine-stitched onto silk, and painted with gold paint. Each image is edged with
colored watercolor paper and embellished with beads.

"Stitch Sample Book" • 13¾" x 10¾"

˙STITCH SAMPLE BOOK˙

Flowers inspired this piece. The main medium is fabric paper with a Tyvek base. The background is accented with vertical lines of machine stitching. The foreground was created with flowers and stems made of colored fabric papers in contrasting colors that were machine-stitched to the background. Sequins and beads embellish the cover.

Now that you've had a chance to read about my different book assembly methods, why not try one? The "Checkerboard Book" on the following pages is a good project to start with.

BOOK PROJECT
'Checkerboard Book'

This is a traditional-style book with stitched signatures. It also includes a gusset that lines the inside front and back covers.

DIRECTIONS

Making the cover wrap

1. Take a square of black velvet slightly smaller than the proposed size of your book and use a stencil to paint a checkerboard of Xpandaprint squares. Heat the Xpandaprint with a heat gun until it puffs up. Allow it to cool and then paint the Xpandaprint with acrylic metallic gold paint and allow to dry. When dry, paint it with patina solution and allow it to dry again. Finally, apply gold leaf with gold leaf adhesive.

2. Take torn squares from pages of old text and paint with diluted acrylic paint. Glue these squares, layering them on top of each other, in the vacant squares of the checkerboard. Use enough layers to equal the depth of the Xpandaprint.

3. For the fleur-de-lis motif, roll out Model Magic with a plastic roller to the desired thickness. Apply talcum powder to the surface of the stamp and press the stamp into the Model Magic. Remove the stamp and allow the Model Magic to dry overnight. Make as many stampings as you need to cover each of the stacked text squares. When dry, cut out the fleur-de-lis images with a scissors or sharp knife and paint with diluted acrylic paint. Allow the paint to dry and then rub with metallic rub-ons. Glue the finished motifs to the squares of old text.

4. Stack a small, star-shaped button on top of a large mother-of-pearl button and stitch through both buttons to attach them to the finished surface of the Xpandaprint squares, repeating as necessary to cover each square.

5. Take a piece of black velvet large enough to cover the front, back, and spine of the book, plus approximately 1" all around. Place the prepared checkerboard covering on top of the larger piece, positioning it on the right side so that it will be centered on the front cover when the book is assembled. Then machine-stitch the prepared covering to the larger piece.

Cover

1. Cut 2 squares of mat board to make the front and rear covers and cut a strip for the spine.

2. Glue batting to one side of each piece of mat board. Glue the mat board, batting-side-down, onto the wrong side of the velvet covering. Leave narrow gaps (approximately $\frac{1}{8}$") between the spine and the front and back covers. This should leave a margin of velvet approximately 1" wide around the full cover (back, front, and spine).

3. Fold the velvet over the cover at each corner and glue down. Fold the velvet margins over the cover (top, bottom, and sides) and glue down, trimming at the corners to avoid a build-up of layers.

Signatures (pages)

1. Fold sheets of watercolor paper into signatures of the desired size.

2. With an awl, make 5 holes, equally spaced, in the fold of each signature, starting 1" in from the top and bottom edges of the paper.

3. Using another sheet of watercolor paper, form an inner lining for the cover by making 2 folds at the center of the sheet to form a gusset equal to the width of the spine. The liner piece, when folded, should be long enough to cover the spine and pages completely.

4. Take the awl and make holes in the gusset for each of the signatures (e.g. if you have 2 signatures you would have 10 holes in the gusset, 2 rows of 5, side by side).

5. Stitch the signatures to the gusset. When all signatures are stitched in place, glue the inner lining to the inside of the book cover.

Finishing

Cut strips of chiffon and hand-stitch them, with beads, to the front cover to hide the machine stitching where you attached the front panel. Cut another strip of chiffon and attach it to the spine in the same manner. Embellish the spine with buttons and beads hand-stitched to the chiffon strip.

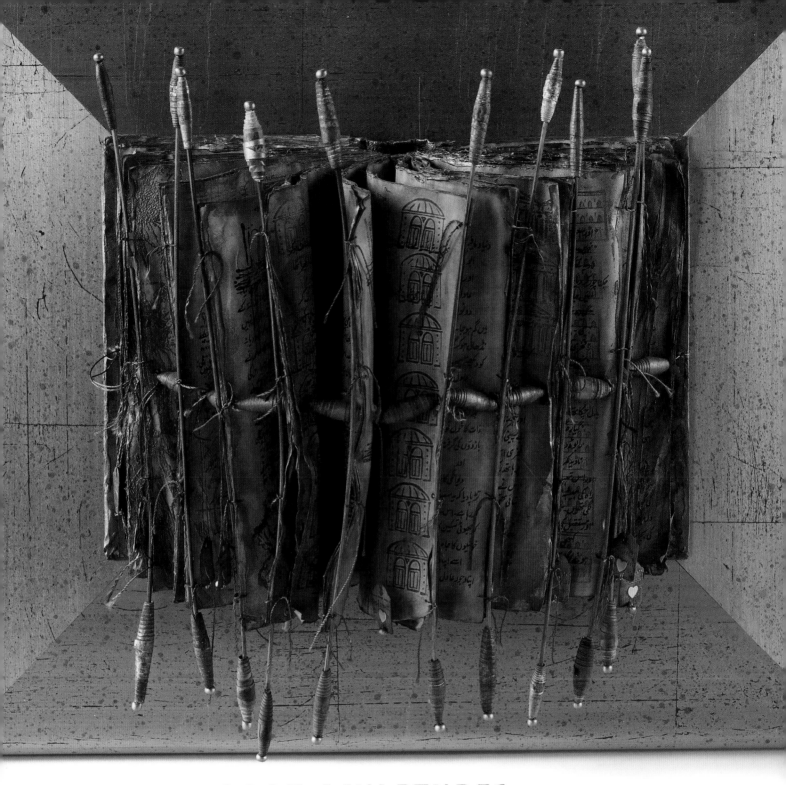

"Fandango" • *13½" x 16¼"*

BOOK SCULPTURES

In addition to making books that you can "read" or use, I also enjoy creating book sculptures that stand on their own as home or office décor.

'FANDANGO'

The pages of this book were dyed with a variety of colors and glued together in blocks of 8 - 10 pages. The pages were then rubber-stamped with images. Canes were stitched to the edges of the page blocks and decorated with handmade paper beads and gold bead finials. A thread was passed through each page block at the center and handmade paper-bead separators were inserted on the thread to space the blocks. Finally, the book was inset into a frame for wall-mounting.

"Bookstack" • *13" x 9 ½" x 8 ½"*

˙BOOKSTACK˙

This sculpture is composed of nine books that have been individually dyed in different colors, glued together in a spiraling stack, and mounted on a wooden platform with ball feet. The top book is decorated with text, rubber-stamped images, tags, buttons, beads, and letters. The bookmark is made from ribbon, cord, tags, beads, buttons, and tassels.

❧ RESOURCES ❧

Alpha Stamps
www.alphastamps.com
Stamps

Bernina®
www.bernina.com

Dharma Trading
www.dharmatrading.com
800-542-5227
Dye supplies

Dick Blick
www.dickblick.com
800-828-4548
*Dip pens, Friendly Plastic,
Gesso, Pebeo gel*

Fire Mountain Gems
1 Fire Mountain Way
Grants Pass, OR 97526-2373
www.firemountaingems.com
Beads

Invoke Arts
1036 ½ Chorro St.
San Luis Obispo, CA 93401
805-541-5197
www.invokearts.com
Rubber stamps

Jacquard® Paints
www.jacquardproducts.com
800-442-0455
Lumiere™ paints

Joggles
www.joggles.com
(Internet orders only)
*Hot water-soluble fabric, Pellon,®
Kunin felt*

Meinke Toy
www.meinketoy.com
*Hot water-soluble fabric,
Xpandaprint*

100 Proof Press
www.100proofpress.com
740-594-2315
Rubber stamps

Quiltingarts, LLC
www.quiltingartsllc.com
866-698-6989
*Rubber stamps, Shiva Paintstiks,
books, magazines*

Ranger Ink
www.rangerink.com
800-244-2211
Pigment Inks and dye-based inks

Stamp Diva
www.stampdiva.com
Rubber stamps

Stampers Anonymous
3110 Payne Ave.
Cleveland, OH 44114
800-945-3980
www.stampersanonymous.com
Rubber stamps

Thai silks
252 State St.
Dept. QA
Los Altos, CA 94022
www.thaisilks.com
Silk fabrics

The Thread Studio (Australia)
www.thethreadstudio.com
61 89227 1561
*Xpandaprint and other
mixed-media supplies*

Utrecht Art
6 Corporate Drive
Cranbury, NJ 08512
609-409-8001
www.utrecht.com
Paints, brushes, paper/board

Volcano Arts
www.volcanoarts.biz
209-296-6535
*Metallic rub-ons and
bookmaking supplies*

United Kingdom

ArtVanGo
www.artvango.co.uk
01 438 814946
*Gesso, Japanese paper, Lokta Paper,
Metal shim, Mulberry paper, Pebeo
gel, watercolor paper, Procion Dye
and Deka Dyes, Tyvek®,
Xpandaprint*

City & Guilds
1 Giltspur Street
London EC1A 9DD
United Kingdom
enquiry@cityandguilds.com
020 7294 2800
Fax: 020 7294 2400

Impressive Images
22 Green Drive,
Timperley, Altrincham,
Cheshire, WA15 6JW
U. K.
0161 980 1732
impressiveimages2004
@yahoo.com
*Mail order rubber
stamp company*

Opus School of Textile Arts
20 Crown Street
Harrow on the Hill
Middlesex
HA2 0HR
United Kingdom
www.opus-online.co.uk
44 (0) 20 8864 7283

Stef Francis
www.stef-francis.co.uk
01803 323004
*Fine perle cotton, 6-strand cotton,
fine and medium-thick silk threads,
Silk Noil*

Books

COVER TO COVER
by Shereen LaPlantz
Lark Books, NY
ISBN 0-937274-87-9
Paperback, $16.95

THE ART & CRAFT
OF HANDMADE BOOKS
by Shereen Plantz
Lark Books, NY
ISBN 1579904386
Paperback, $17.95

UNIQUE HANDMADE BOOKS
by Alisa Golden
Sterling Publishers, NY
ISBN 1402706146
Paperback, $17.95

Beryl Taylor was born in Rotherham, England, and grew up in the Manchester area where, after showing artistic talent, she studied at the Manchester High School of Art. She spent many years as a wife, mother, and nurse until her artistic leanings were reawakened when she discovered creative embroidery. She trained at the City & Guilds textile and embroidery program and later started the textile group Threadmill with other City & Guilds graduates.

Beryl moved to the United States from England with her family in 2002 and now devotes all of her time to her art. She imaginatively manipulates, dyes, paints, stamps, embroiders, and decorates her papers and fabrics to produce enriching textured effects and vibrant colors. An enduring theme in Beryl's work is the incorporation of the heart motif which is, in her own words, a reflection of her love for her art. Beryl is currently living and working as a mixed-media artist in Monroe Township, New Jersey. She can be contacted at berylptaylor@aol.com.